WALT'S DISNEYLAND

It's Still There
If You Know Where to Look

Jim Denney

Writing in Overdrive Books

Anaheim, California

Jim Denney
Writing in Overdrive Books
P. O. Box 28334
Anaheim CA 92809-8334

Cover design by The Wordsmith.

First Edition: May 2017

Visit the author on the World Wide Web:
WaltsDisneyland.Wordpress.com
and **WritingInOverdrive.com**

Email the author at **Jim@WritingInOverdrive.com**.

Follow Jim Denney on Twitter at
@WaltsDisneyland and **@WriterJimDenney**

Other books by Jim Denney:

Writing in Overdrive
Write Fearlessly
Muse of Fire
Quit Your Day Job
Answers to Satisfy the Soul

The Timebenders science-fantasy series for young readers:
Battle Before Time
Doorway to Doom
Invasion of the Time Troopers
Lost in Cydonia

Disneyland entrance on Harbor Boulevard, 1974.
(Photo: Werner Weiss, courtesy Orange County Archives)

"Disneyland is often called a magic kingdom because it combines fantasy and history, adventure and learning, together with every variety of recreation and fun designed to appeal to everyone."

Walt Disney

Contents

Preface and Dedication

I can't remember a world without Disneyland.

I was not quite two years old when the *Disneyland* TV show premiered October 27, 1954, eight and a half months before the Park opened. The series aired Wednesday nights on ABC. Like the original Disneyland, the show was divided into four lands — Fantasyland, Frontierland, Adventureland, and Tomorrowland. It featured classic Disney films, original dramas, miniseries, and nature documentaries, each episode connected to one of the four lands of Disneyland.

Our family watched *Disneyland* every week. One day in August 1957, we piled into the car and *went* there. I still remember the thrill of walking into Disneyland for the first time. There I was, looking wide-eyed down Main Street toward Sleeping Beauty Castle — exactly as I had seen it on my TV screen at home. I could hardly believe it was real.

Though I was not even five years old, Disneyland was a feast for my imagination. Where else could I explore caves on Tom Sawyer Island in the morning, blast off for the Moon at noon, then soar over Never Land before dinner? If your imagination is in good working order, you'll board the Disneyland Trolley and *believe* you're rumbling down Main Street USA circa 1910.

I never met Walt Disney. Not knowingly, anyway. It's possible, however, that I met him and didn't recognize him. That often happened in Disneyland's early days.

My brother Tim and me (I'm on the left) in the Disneyland Dog Pound, August 1957.

During one of my boyhood pilgrimages to Disneyland, I asked my dad if we might see Walt himself at the Park. Dad said, "I doubt it, son. A busy man like Mr. Disney doesn't have a lot of time to spend at Disneyland." That was one of the few times my father was ever wrong.

Fact is, in those days, Walt spent a lot of time at the Park, observing people, talking to his guests, listening to their unguarded remarks, gauging their reactions. He sometimes put on a striped jacket and straw hat, serving sundaes and cones at the Carnation Ice Cream Parlor. Other times, guests spotted Walt at the throttle of one of the Santa Fe & Disneyland Railroad trains. And yes, Walt waited in line along with his guests, so he could hear what people were saying about his Park.

Walt Disney lived for days or weeks at a time in his apartment over the Fire House on Main Street. In many ways, Walt is still there in his Park, still making sure everything is neat and pretty, making sure the Park sparkles like the golden spires of his Castle. Walt promised us that Disneyland would keep changing, keep growing, and it has. But he also promised us that the optimistic, adventurous spirit of Disneyland would *never* change — another promise kept.

I wrote this book to uncover those parts of Disneyland that have remained essentially unchanged since Walt left us in December 1966. If you know where to look, Walt's Disneyland is still there, waiting to be discovered and enjoyed.

In the process of researching and writing this book, I have tried to be as thorough and accurate as possible. This isn't easy, because so many myths have grown up around Walt Disney. He encouraged some of those myths himself. Though Walt was a man of strong principles and dependable integrity, he was also a storyteller who was not averse to making a good story even better.

Disney historian (and former Disneyland cast member) Jason Schultz points out, "It wasn't really until at least twenty-five years after the Park opened that a historical consciousness about it developed. . . . Our knowledge of what really happened will always be limited. . . . Our yearning for a good story frequently gets the better of us."[1]

I love a good story as much as anybody — but I also want to get as close to the truth as I can. So if you find any inaccuracies in this book, please write and tell me so I can correct them in the next edition. (You'll find my contact information on the copyright page.)

Among the many gifts my father and mother gave me were a love of good storytelling, a fascination with the past, and an optimistic outlook on the future. One of the ways they encouraged these traits was by taking me to Disneyland at an early age.

So I gratefully dedicate this book to my father and mother, Lee and Twyla Denney. Thank you, Dad and Mom, for filling my eyes with wonder, and giving me my first unforgettable experience of Walt's Disneyland.

JIM DENNEY
Main Street USA
March 9, 2017

Introduction

"I was walking down a street in Beverly Hills and a man passed by with so many gifts he couldn't seem to hold them all. And then I saw it was Walt Disney!"
—*Ray Bradbury*[1]

In March 2005, our family went to the Performing Arts Center in Duarte, east of Pasadena, to meet one of my literary heroes, Ray Bradbury. He talked about the stories, novels, and screenplays he had written, and about what it takes to achieve our goals and make our dreams come true.

I had corresponded with Ray a few times and had spoken with him on the phone, but this was my first time meeting him in person. After his talk, our family went up and I gave him my copy of *The Martian Chronicles* to sign. I told him he had inspired me to become a writer, and I mentioned *How to Be Like Walt*, the book on Walt Disney I had co-written with Pat Williams, co-founder of the Orlando Magic.

Ray's eyes lit up. "Oh, yes! A wonderful book! Your friend sent me a copy. Let me tell you how I met Walt."

I looked down and saw that he had signed "Ray" in my book, but had stopped in mid-autograph. I already knew the story of his encounter with Walt — we had told it in the book — but what a gift for Ray to share it with me in person. "I'd love to hear it," I said.

Ray Bradbury (Photo: Alan Light)

Ray smiled, thinking back. "I was Christmas shopping in Beverly Hills. I saw a man coming toward me, his arms loaded with presents. I said, 'That's Walt Disney!'

"I rushed up to him and said, 'Mr. Disney?' He said, 'Yes?' I said, 'I'm Ray Bradbury, and I love your movies.' He said, 'Oh, Ray Bradbury! I know your books.' I said, 'Thank God!' And he said, 'Why?' I said, 'Because I'd love to take you to lunch sometime.' And Walt said, 'How about tomorrow?'

"Isn't that beautiful? 'How about tomorrow?' Not next month, not someday soon — tomorrow. Walt Disney was spontaneous. The very next day, I was in his office in Burbank, and we had lunch — soup and sandwiches on an old card table. We talked and talked, and I told him how much I loved Disneyland. He was thrilled to hear it."

After telling me this story, Ray looked down at my half-signed copy of *The Martian Chronicles*. Then he wrote "Bradbury," completing his signature. I thanked him and I was happy.

In 1965, Ray Bradbury penned an appreciation of Walt for *Holiday* magazine. Bradbury recalled that, at age twelve, he owned the first Mickey Mouse buttons in town. At nineteen, he worried that he might not live to see the premiere of *Fantasia*. By age forty-five, he had seen *Fantasia* fifteen times in the theater, *Snow White* a dozen times, and *Pinocchio* eight times. "I was," he said, "and still am, a Disney nut."

Ray Bradbury visited Disneyland for the first time with actor Charles Laughton, who played Captain Bligh in the 1935 version of *Mutiny on the Bounty*. Bradbury said he cherished the day his actor friend dragged him through the gates of Disneyland. Laughton, he recalled, "plowed a furrow in the mobs; he surged ahead, one great all-enveloping presence from whom all fell aside."

First stop: The Jungle Cruise. "We made straight for the nearest boat," Bradbury recalled. "Charlie sat near the prow, pointing here to crocodiles, there to bull elephants, farther on to feasting lions. He laughed at the wild palaver of our river-boat steersman's jokes, ducked when pistols were fired dead-on at charging hippopotamuses, and basked face-up in the rain, eyes shut, as we sailed under the Schweitzer Falls."

Then Ray's love of the future drew them to Tomorrowland: "We blasted off in another boat," he recalled, "this one of the future, the Rocket to the Moon."

Next stop: Frontierland. "We circuited the Mississippi in the *Mark Twain*, with the jazz band thumping like a great dark heart, and the steamboat blowing its forlorn dragon-voice whistle, and the slow banks passing."

At day's end, Charlie and Ray, two weary grownup children, climbed into their car and headed home with "Charlie the greatest child and most weary of all."[2]

That's the way to tour Disneyland, with a complete suspension of disbelief, with a drunken sense of joy and eyes wide with wonder. Let the child inside you come out and play. Laugh and shout! Plunge into the mind and soul of Walt Disney.

After Walt's death, The Walt Disney Company hired Ray Bradbury to contribute ideas and a narration script for the iconic Spaceship Earth attraction in Florida's Walt Disney World. Bradbury said he wanted to include many ideas he and Walt had talked about during their friendship.

In gratitude for his contributions, Disneyland honored Ray Bradbury with a decorated oak tree, named after his novel *The Halloween Tree*. Disneyland's Halloween Tree is located in Frontierland. It was dedicated on Halloween night, 2007, and is decorated every Halloween season.

The Halloween Tree

Bradbury said his first impression of Walt Disney was of a man "with so many gifts he couldn't seem to hold them all." Bradbury was referring to Christmas gifts — yet it's a fitting description of Walt Disney himself. Throughout his life, Walt had more gifts than he could hold — not just gifts of talent and imagination, but gifts of generosity and love for the human race.

Disneyland is one of Walt's gifts to you and me. Come wish upon a star. Spend a day on the other side of the looking glass. May all your dreams come true.

"Walt Disney's Disneyland liberates men to be their better selves."
—*Ray Bradbury*

CHAPTER ONE

The Walt Disney Story

"Everybody in the world was once a child. So in planning a new picture, we don't think of grown-ups, and we don't think of children, but just of that fine, clean, unspoiled spot down deep in every one of us that maybe the world has made us forget and that maybe our pictures can help recall."
—Walt Disney

Disneyland really began," Walt said, "when my two daughters were very young. Saturday was always Daddy's Day, and I would take them to the merry-go-round and sit on a bench eating peanuts while they rode. And sitting there, alone, I felt there should be something built, some kind of family park where parents and children could have fun together."[1]

Walt did dream of Disneyland as he sat on that bench in Griffith Park — but that's not where his dreams of Disneyland truly began. A news story published in the *Long Beach Independent-Press-Telegram*, Friday, July 15, 1955 (two days before Disneyland's grand opening), stated that files in Disney's Burbank studio archives contained "original Disneyland sketches, bearing the 1932 date." Those sketches were dated *a full year* before his first daughter Diane was born.

Display in the foyer of the Main Street Opera House at Disneyland. The inscription on the bench reads: "The actual park bench from the Griffith Park Merry-Go-Round in Los Angeles, where Walt Disney first dreamed of Disneyland." (Photo: Sam Howzit)[2]

The dream of Disneyland existed long before Walt was a father. In fact, Disneyland was born in the heart and soul of a little boy growing up in middle America. When you walk down Main Street USA, or cross the drawbridge into Fantasyland, or journey through time and space in Tomorrowland, you're exploring the memories and dreams of a young Missouri farm boy.

Today it's hard to imagine a world without Disneyland. But when Walt was planning his Park, financial analysts and entertainment experts predicted failure. "I could never convince the financiers that Disneyland was feasible," he once said, "because dreams offer too little collateral." To build it, Walt had to bet his studio and his personal fortune. Had Disneyland failed, he would have been ruined, personally and professionally.

By sheer persistence, Walt willed Disneyland into being. He was not building an amusement park. He was building a dream. The dream had been a part of him ever since he first set eyes on a place called Electric Park.

A Return to Childhood

Walter Elias Disney was born in Chicago on December 5, 1901, the youngest of four sons born to Elias and Flora Disney; his little sister Ruth was born in 1903. Walt's father was an unimaginative man with an austere temperament. Even so, Elias Disney loved his family. He had no vices, such as drinking or gambling, and he sacrificed his own wants and needs to provide for his family. Though young Walt had his share of conflict with his father, and resented Elias Disney's rigid attitudes, he loved and respected his father.

Elias taught Walt and his siblings the importance of hard work, perseverance, integrity, and a good reputation. Elias also set an example of compassion and caring for one's fellow man, and he frequently offered free room and board to strangers who were down on their luck. "I had tremendous respect for him," Walt once said. "I worshipped him. Nothing but his family counted."

Flora Disney, Walt's mother, was an even-tempered woman, the daughter of a scholar. She taught Walt how to read before he attended kindergarten.

Walt had no memory of those early years in Chicago. When he was four years old, Elias moved the family out of the big city and onto a farm just outside of Marceline, Missouri. Walt's earliest and happiest memories were those of a Midwestern farm boy growing up near a small American town.

Disneyland's Main Street USA is an idealized and romanticized version of Marceline — the place Walt always considered his hometown. What makes Marceline special is that there is nothing special about it. The town is exactly like countless other small American towns from California to Maine. Harper Goff, the Disney designer who created Main Street USA under Walt's direction, based his drawings on his own hometown, Fort Collins, Colorado. When Walt saw Goff's designs, he said Main Street USA was just like the Marceline of his memories.

I spent my earliest years in an identical small town in the 1950s — Coalinga, California. The streets and storefronts looked just like those on Main Street USA. When I lived there, no one ever locked their doors at night. Crime was unknown. The small-town America of Walt's memories was no myth. It existed, and I lived there, too.

In 1949, as Walt was becoming increasingly serious about building his nostalgic, futuristic dream park, the Disney Studio released a movie aptly titled *So Dear to My Heart*. It tells the story of a young boy growing up on a farm near a small Indiana town on a railroad line, much like Marceline. Walt later said that the film was "especially close to me. Why, that's the life my brother and I grew up with as kids out in Missouri."[3]

Walt only lived on that farm near Marceline for four years, but his brief time as a Missouri farm boy defined him. The animals on the farm were his friends and companions. He knew each one by name and he invented stories about their adventures. One pudgy little piglet (named Skinny) followed young Walt like a puppy.

Walt's imagination feasted on rural and small-town life. When a circus parade came to Marceline, young Walt was there, sitting on the curb with his mother and sister, watching the clowns, acrobats, and elephants pass by. His parents couldn't afford admission to the big top, so Walt went home, fashioned a circus tent out of burlap sacks, and charged his friends 10 cents a head to see the pets and farm animals he had penned up inside. His mother made him refund every dime.

(Today, you can experience Walt's love of the circus aboard Dumbo the Flying Elephant and the Casey Jr. Circus Train at Disneyland.)

Marceline was established by the Santa Fe Railroad as a coaling and watering stop for its steam-powered trains. Walt's uncle Mike Martin was a Santa Fe engineer who often stopped by the farm to sit on the porch, and tell Walt stories of his adventures on the rails.

Walt never got over his fascination with trains. Before building the Disneyland Railroad, he built a one-eighth-scale miniature live-steam railroad on a half mile of track behind his home in the Holmby Hills district of Los Angeles. He called it the Carolwood Pacific Railroad, naming it after his address at 355 N. Carolwood Drive. The track looped around the house, passed through a tunnel, and crossed a forty-six-foot trestle.

Walt also built a backyard barn as a workshop for his model railroad — an exact replica of the barn where he'd spent many happy hours on the farm near Marceline. Walt's Carolwood Barn was later moved to Griffith Park, Los Angeles, where it now serves as a Disney museum.

Main Street USA and the Disneyland Railroad were more than a tribute to a simpler time. They were Walt's time machine to the joys of his childhood.

Electric Memories

During his boyhood in Marceline, Walt saw his first stage play, a touring performance of *Peter Pan*. Young Walt was struck by the ability of actors to create magic before an audience. From his earliest days, he was caught up in a world of imagination, storytelling, and illusions.

In 1909, the Disney farm was failing and Elias was seriously ill. He sold the farm for much less than he paid, and prepared to move his family a hundred miles away, to Kansas City. Eight-year-old Walt wept bitterly as the auctioneers sold off his beloved farm animals.

Elias used the proceeds to buy a newspaper distributorship in Kansas City. He put Walt and his brother Roy to work delivering newspapers without pay. Walt and Roy rose every morning at 3:30, often wading through waist-high snowdrifts to deliver their papers. Walt would get to school at 9:00 and sometimes fall asleep in class. After school, he worked at a corner candy store. He formed an intense work ethic at an early age.

The Marceline years — some of the happiest years of Walt's life — were over. His Kansas City years were *literally* the stuff of nightmares. As an adult, Walt suffered recurring bad dreams of trudging through blizzards or being punished by his father for a missed delivery.

But Walt's Kansas City years also unleashed his passion for performing. On Lincoln's birthday, when Walt was in the fifth grade, he came to school dressed as Honest Abe — topcoat, stovepipe hat, beard, and all. He recited the Gettysburg address and his classmates applauded. He also entertained friends with impressions of silent film star Charlie Chaplin, or by telling stories that he illustrated on the chalkboard.

Kansas City's Electric Park at night — Walt's inspiration.

Young Walt Disney was influenced by a huge amusement park at 46th Street and the Paseo, a fifteen-block streetcar ride from Walt's Kansas City home. Known as Electric Park, it was built by Joseph Heim of the Heim Brothers Brewery in 1907, and remained in operation until 1925, when it was destroyed by fire.

Electric Park featured band concerts, ballroom dancing, vaudeville shows, penny arcades, shooting galleries, a carousel, a huge indoor swimming pool, cafés, souvenir shops, flat-bottomed boats that would "shoot the chutes" into a lagoon, a wooden roller coaster, and a carnival midway with thrill rides. A steam train ran around the park, and a fireworks show lit up the summer nights.

Unlike most amusement parks of the time, Electric Park was clean and well-maintained. Walt often spoke of Electric Park's influence on his design of Disneyland, saying that Disneyland "has that thing — the imagination and the feeling of happy excitement — I knew when I was a kid."[4]

Electric Park was named for the 100,000 electric lights that transformed the park into a fairyland at night. Visit Disneyland at night, and you'll rediscover the incandescent glories of that lost Kansas City park, as remembered by Walt Disney.

Walt lived in this house at 3028 Bellefontaine Avenue, Kansas City, from 1914 to 1917, and again from 1919 to 1921. (Photo: Missouri Department of Natural Resources / Landmarks Commission, taken in 1977)

When Walt was fifteen, his father moved back to Chicago, taking Flora and Walt's sister Ruth with him. Walt and two of his brothers remained in Kansas City. Walt sold newspapers, candy, and tobacco on the Santa Fe Railroad, and the engineer often let Walt ride in the cab and blow the steam whistle.

Walt later joined his parents and sister in Chicago, where he attended McKinley High School by day and the Academy of Fine Arts at night. His art instructor, Carl Wertz, admired Walt's comedic drawings and encouraged his ambition to become a cartoonist.

Started by a Mouse

During the summer of 1918, sixteen-year-old Walt enlisted with the American Ambulance Corps of the Red Cross (he fudged his birthdate by a year to qualify). Walt's Red Cross training was interrupted by a bout of Spanish influenza — the infamous 1918 flu epidemic that killed from 20 to 50 million people worldwide. Walt shipped out to France on November 18 — a week after World War I ended.

In France, Walt chauffeured military officers and delivered relief supplies. In September 1919, Walt's Red Cross unit was disbanded and he returned to Kansas City, hoping to become a newspaper cartoonist.

In 1920, nineteen-year-old Walt and his friend Ub Iwerks formed Iwerks-Disney Commercial Artists. Walt met Iwerks while working at an advertising company in Kansas City. Later, Walt, Ub Iwerks, and animator Fred Harman began a cartoon series called Laugh-O-Grams, based on fairy tales and Aesop's fables. Laugh-O-Grams became popular, as did Walt's next animated series, the

Alice Comedies. But Walt was not a good money manager, and soon went bankrupt.

*In 1919, Walt started working at Kansas City Film Ad Com-
pany, where he met Ub Iwerks. Walt's boss, A. V. Cauger, let
him take a company movie camera home. In this garage behind
the Disney home on Bellefontaine, Walt, Ub, and other friends
experimented with animation. (Photo: Missouri Department of
Natural Resources / Landmarks Commission, taken in 1977)*

Walt moved to Hollywood, California, and started
over. This time, he had his brother, Roy O. Disney, to
supply the hard-headed business acumen he lacked. The
Disney Brothers' Studio was located on Hyperion Avenue
in the Silver Lake district of Los Angeles. In 1925, Walt
hired Lillian Bounds as an ink and paint artist. On July
25, 1925, following a whirlwind courtship, Walt and
Lillian were married.

When the Alice Comedies had run their course, Walt
launched a new character, Oswald the Lucky Rabbit,

drawn by Ub Iwerks. In February 1928, Walt and Lillian took a train to New York to negotiate with distributor Charles Mintz for more money. Mintz offered Walt a pay *cut* instead — and he threatened to steal Disney's animators and shut him down.

Walt couldn't believe his animators would betray him. He called Roy and told him of Mintz's threat. Roy investigated and learned that Mintz had lured away all of Walt's artists except Iwerks and two assistant animators, Johnny Cannon and Les Clark. Walt lost most of his animation staff — and he lost Oswald.

(A side note: In 2006, The Walt Disney Company made one of the most unusual trades in business history. Disney, the parent company of the ABC television network, had sportscaster Al Michaels under contract. Meanwhile, NBC/Universal owned the rights to Oswald the Lucky Rabbit. Almost eighty years after Walt lost the rights to Oswald, the company he founded reacquired Oswald in a trade that sent Al Michaels to NBC. When Michaels learned he'd been traded for a cartoon character, he said, "I'm going to be a trivia answer someday."[5] Oswald now makes personal appearances on Buena Vista Street at Disney California Adventure.)

Though Walt had been cheated by Charles Mintz and betrayed by his own animators, he remained optimistic. He still had Ub Iwerks and he had his ideas. So Walt sent Roy a telegram:

LEAVING TONITE STOPPING OVER KC
ARRIVE HOME SUNDAY MORNING SEVEN THIRTY
DON'T WORRY EVERYTHING OK
WILL GIVE DETAILS WHEN ARRIVE
WALT

Walt and Lillian boarded the 20th Century Limited at Grand Central Station and began their journey home. Along the way, Walt pondered ideas for the future. One of those ideas was an adventurous mouse named Mickey.

In October 1931, three years after Mickey's debut, Walt authored an article in *Windsor Magazine*, published in England. He recalled:

> Why did I choose a mouse for my principal character? Principally because I needed a small animal. I couldn't use a rabbit, because there already was a rabbit on the screen. So I decided upon a mouse, as I have always thought they were very interesting little creatures. At first I decided to call him Mortimer Mouse, but changed his name to Mickey as the name has a more friendly sound, and Mickey really is a friendly sort of character. We have become great pals, Mickey and I. And I'm not fooling when I say that he is just as much a person to me as anyone I know. He is full of vitality and youth, and has the most endearing childlike ways. He is unassuming and modest — not at all like all those temperamental film stars we hear so much about!
>
> While returning from a visit to New York, I plotted out the first story. . . .[6]

Walt later called Mickey Mouse "a symbol of independence." In a 1948 interview, he recalled:

> [Mickey] popped out of my mind onto a drawing pad twenty years ago on a train ride from Manhattan to Hollywood at a time when business fortunes of my brother Roy and myself were at lowest ebb

and disaster seemed right around the corner. Born of necessity, the little fellow literally freed us of immediate worry. He provided the means for expanding our organization to its present dimensions and for extending the medium of cartoon animation toward new entertainment levels. He spelled production liberation for us.[7]

On Sunday, March 18, 1928, the 20th Century Limited pulled into Pasadena station. Ub Iwerks and Roy Disney were there to greet Walt and Lillian. Stepping off the train, Walt said, "We lost Oswald, but we're going to start a new series with a new character." They went to Walt's home, where Walt told Ub and Roy all about Mickey Mouse. Ub and his assistants would work in secret. Walt would supply the stories, and his small, loyal staff would animate them.

The first Mickey cartoon Walt released, *Steamboat Willie*, featured a new sound-synchronization technology called Cinephone (it was the third Mickey cartoon produced, after *Plane Crazy* and *The Gallopin' Gaucho*). Mickey Mouse was an instant sensation, quickly overtaking Felix the Cat in popularity. By the early 1930s, Mickey's fame had spread worldwide.

Walt's daughter Diane Disney Miller said that her father saw Mickey as an extension of his own personality. "He did Mickey's voice for years," she said, "and as Mickey became more of a celebrity, there was a distinct change in [Mickey's] character and his behavior." In the early cartoons, Mickey did "almost vulgar things," she said, but after Mickey became the symbol of the company, Walt and his staff "invented Donald Duck and Goofy to do all those things."[8]

Mickey was a key factor in the creation and success of Disneyland. As Walt once said, "I only hope that we never lose sight of one thing — that it was all started by a mouse."[9]

The Dream Gathers Steam

Walt began planning a full-length animated feature, *Snow White and the Seven Dwarfs*, in 1934. Industry experts and film critics quickly dubbed it "Disney's Folly" and predicted disaster. Roy and Lillian tried to talk him out of it. But Walt had already experienced bankruptcy early in his life, and he wasn't afraid of big risks.

Walt in a promotional trailer for
Snow White and the Seven Dwarfs *(1937).*

Snow White took three years to produce. Had it failed, the Disney Studio would have been finished. But when "Disney's Folly" premiered at the Carthay Circle Theater on December 21, 1937, critics raved and audiences mobbed the theater. The success of *Snow White* boosted

Walt's confidence in his own judgment. He'd need that confidence for his riskiest project of all: Disneyland.

The success of *Snow White* gave Walt the capital to build his new studio in Burbank, which opened for business on Christmas Eve, 1939. From his new studio, Walt launched the Golden Age of Animation with such classic films as *Pinocchio, Fantasia, Bambi*, and *Dumbo*. The studio continued turning out high-quality shorts starring Mickey Mouse, Donald Duck, Pluto, and Goofy.

In 1941, the Screen Cartoonists' Guild organized a strike that strangled production at the studio. Once again, Walt felt betrayed. His artists worked under the best conditions for the highest pay in the industry. Why were they striking? Walt needed to get away from the studio and its problems. He accepted an invitation from the State Department to tour Latin America as a good-will ambassador, leaving Roy to settle the strike.

During the post-War years, Disney produced films that would provide the themes for Walt's theme park — *Make Mine Music* (1946, featuring a musical segment called "Blue Bayou"), *The Adventures of Ichabod and Mr. Toad* (1949, which inspired Mr. Toad's Wild Ride), *Alice in Wonderland* (1951, the inspiration for both the Alice in Wonderland dark ride and The Mad Tea Party attraction), and *Peter Pan* (1953, the inspiration for Peter Pan's Flight).

Walt's amusement park dreams were constantly on his mind during the late 1940s. He visited a number of amusement parks, including Beverly Park at Beverly and La Cienega — a modest but clean place with a merry-go-round, a waterless boat ride (the boats moved on wheels), and a small train that ran around the park.

Walt sat on a bench, occasionally asking the children which rides they enjoyed the most.

Andy Russell, Walt Disney, and Dinah Shore in a promotional still for Make Mine Music *(1946).*

For years, the dream of a Disney-themed amusement park had been in the back of his mind. Finally, in the summer of 1948, Walt knew it was time to get serious about building his dream.

CHAPTER TWO

Walt's Dream Becomes Reality

"Disneyland is something that will never be finished. It's something that I can keep developing. . . . A [motion] picture is a thing, once you wrap it up and turn it over to Technicolor, you're through. Snow White *is a dead issue with me. But I can change the Park, because it's alive."*
—*Walt Disney*

In 1948, when Walt told his brother about his plans to build Disneyland (or Mickey Mouse Park, as he then called it), Roy went apoplectic, calling it a "screwball idea." Walt's wife Lillian also opposed it. So did the Disney board of directors.

Walt later recalled, "I had a little dream for Disneyland adjoining the studio. I couldn't get anybody to go along with me because we were going through this financial depression. But I kept working on it, and I worked on it with my own money. Not the studio's money, my own money."[1]

On August 31, 1948, Walt wrote a memo to Disney production designer Dick Kelsey, describing a detailed and fully formed vision of the Park:

The Main Village, which includes the Railroad Station, is built around a village green or informal park. In the park will be benches, a bandstand, drinking fountain, trees, and shrubs. It will be a place for people to sit and rest; mothers and grandmothers can watch over small children at play. I want it to be very relaxing, cool, and inviting.

Around the park will be built the town. At one end will be the Railroad Station; at the other end, the Town Hall. The Hall will be built to represent a Town Hall, but actually we will use it as our administration building. It will be the headquarters of the entire project.[2]

Walt went on to describe many other features of his vision for Mickey Mouse Park: Disney-themed carnival rides. A carousel or merry-go-round. A Wild West frontier town, complete with cowboys, a stagecoach, and a saloon-style theater. A scale model steam-powered train to take guests from Mickey Mouse Park, over Riverside Drive, and through the studio complex. A radio and TV broadcast studio. Shops to sell Disney books, dolls, toys, and other souvenirs.

The dream of the Park seized Walt's imagination. "Once he got this bug about the Park, it was an obsession," animator Ward Kimball recalled. "That's all he thought about. I was in on the very beginning of that, because he started with his interest in the railroad. . . . I think the nurse and his doctor said he needed a hobby."[3]

Disneyland was destined to become the most expensive "hobby" in history.

From Mickey Mouse Park to Walt's Kingdom

The longer Walt pondered his idea, the bigger it grew. Soon, he realized the vacant lot across the street couldn't contain his dream. He was no longer planning an amusement park. He had begun to envision a magic kingdom with a castle that towered over realms of the past, future, and pure imagination. Rumbling around the borders of Walt's kingdom, like a cast-iron specter from the past, was a steam-powered train.

Locomotive No. 2, E. P. Ripley, at Main Street Station, June 1960. (Santa Fe Railroad promotional photo)

The dream of Disneyland faced a seemingly insurmountable roadblock: money. Though Disney's post-War movies had done well enough to keep the company solvent, the studio had not enjoyed a blockbuster success since *Dumbo* in 1941.

Walt and Roy argued continually over which direction to take the company. Roy wanted to play it safe and continue making dependably successful feature films — and he wanted Walt to forget about his crazy amusement park notion. Walt wanted to plunge the studio into another ambitious animated feature on the scale of *Snow White*. Just as *Snow White* had enabled him to build his Burbank studio, he believed his next big feature-length success would finance Disneyland.

The movie Walt made was *Cinderella*, based on the fairy tale "Cendrillon" popularized by Charles Perrault in 1697. Featuring lush, richly detailed animation and an unforgettable musical score, *Cinderella* charmed critics and audiences when it released on February 15, 1950. Had the movie failed, the losses might have driven the studio into bankruptcy. But the movie was a hit, both in America and in Europe (a film market that had been closed to Disney during World War II, and was just then making a comeback).

The Walt Disney Studio launched into the 1950s flush with success. Walt was well short of the cash needed to build Disneyland, but he was ready to start drawing up plans. Had it not been for the success of *Cinderella*, Disneyland probably wouldn't exist today.

Walt was a risk-taker, but not a reckless gambler. He believed in prudently assessing every risk. Once he was committed to building Disneyland, Walt hired the Stanford Research Institute to analyze every detail of the Park, from finding the ideal location to calculating the construction costs. Before betting millions on his dream, Walt planned it to the last decimal place.

He also interviewed amusement park operators, telling them he wanted to build a clean, family-friendly park. They laughed at him, telling him he'd go broke trying to hire good people and maintain clean restrooms. Walt decided to follow his own instincts.

In the summer of 1951, Walt and Lillian took a cruise ship to Europe. Walt was scheduled to host the London premiere of *Alice in Wonderland* in July, then tour the continent. After the ship left port, Walt discovered that one of his Holmby Hills neighbors, TV personality Art Linkletter, was aboard the ship with his wife Lois. During the Atlantic crossing, the Disneys and Linkletters became friends and ended up touring Europe together.

One stop on their journey was Tivoli Gardens in Copenhagen, Denmark. Founded in 1843, Tivoli was known for its lush gardens, clean atmosphere, fine restaurants, and nightly fireworks. At night, Tivoli shone with the light from a hundred thousand light bulbs, a sight that reminded Walt of summer nights at Electric Park. Art Linkletter recalled, "As we walked through [Tivoli Gardens], I had my first experience of Walt Disney's childlike delight. . . . He was making notes all the time."[4]

Walt knew that building Disneyland would be the challenge of a lifetime. Even his wife Lillian and brother Roy told him his dreams didn't stand a chance. "Whenever I'd go down and talk to my brother about the Park," Walt later said, "he'd suddenly get busy with financial reports. So I stopped bringing it up."

Leaving Roy out of the loop, Walt began assembling the funds to build Disneyland. He emptied his savings account, borrowed a hundred thousand dollars against his life insurance, sold his Palm Springs vacation home, and borrowed against every scrap of collateral he owned. Yet he knew it was all a drop in the ocean compared to the millions he needed.

During a sleepless night in early 1953, Walt had a flash of inspiration: *Television.*

The medium of television was in its infancy in 1953. World War II had suppressed the growth of television during the early 1940s, but TV had spread rapidly in the late '40s and early '50s. Television technology of the time yielded black and white images that were distorted and ghostly. Yet Walt, a true visionary, understood the power of this new medium to spread excitement about Disneyland from coast to coast.

More important, the three big TV networks had something Walt needed: money. And Walt had something the networks wanted: a vault full of Disney films. He had already produced two live Christmas broadcasts, for NBC in 1950 and CBS in 1951. Why not produce a weekly TV show to raise cash for the Park?

He first took his idea to the two largest networks, NBC and CBS. Both wanted a weekly Disney series, but they wanted nothing to do with Disneyland. So he took his idea to the third-place TV network, the American Broadcasting Company — but ABC turned him down as well.

Walt had struck out. The dream was over — or was it?

Financing the Dream

Walt Disney never cared about money. He once said, "I've always been bored with just making money. I've wanted to do things, I wanted to build things. Get something going. . . . I've only thought of money in one way, and that is to do something with it."[5] Walt was only forced to think about money because his dreams came with such a huge price tag.

In the early 1950s, he averaged four or five hours of sleep per night while brainstorming creative ways to finance his dreams. Some of his unlikeliest ideas proved surprisingly effective. For example, he asked his employees to invest in the Park, starting with his studio nurse, Hazel George. She formed an employees' group, the Disneyland Backers and Boosters. The funds they contributed were tiny compared to the need — but their willingness to invest convinced Roy Disney to reconsider his opposition and finally allocate funds for developing Disneyland.

Walt founded his own company, WED Enterprises (WED stands for Walter Elias Disney; the company is now Walt Disney Imagineering, Inc.). WED Enterprises was dedicated to *imagining* and *engineering* Disneyland, so Walt coined a title for his WED employees, calling them "Imagineers." Walt explained, "We're always exploring and experimenting. . . . We call it Imagineering — the blending of creative imagination and technical know-how."[6] Walt operated WED Enterprises from office space he rented at the Burbank studio. As sole owner of WED Enterprises, he enjoyed not having to consult with Roy on major decisions.

In July 1953, the Stanford Research Institute gave Walt a list of possible sites for the Park. At the top of the list was a sleepy little farming town called Anaheim, located thirty-five miles south of Los Angeles. Though Anaheim was in the middle of nowhere, the Santa Ana Freeway was under construction and would soon link L.A. to Anaheim.

In late 1953, Walt approached the networks again. By this time, Roy was a convert to the cause. The Disney board chose Roy — once Disneyland's most bitter opponent — to pitch the idea to the networks.

Walt worked day and night for forty-eight sleepless hours with artist Herb Ryman to develop an aerial map of Disneyland to show to the network brass. Ryman turned Walt's ideas into a beautifully detailed rendering of Disneyland — the Train Station, the Town Square, Main Street, the Castle, the Rivers of America, the rocket ship in Tomorrowland, all as Walt had foreseen.

The ink on Ryman's artwork was scarcely dry when Roy carried it aboard a plane bound for New York. There he met with executives of NBC and CBS, showing them the artwork and a six-page prospectus on Disneyland. Those meetings, Roy later said, were "exasperating." He explained that the show would be called *Disneyland* — the Park and the show were a package deal. The network execs continued to say they wanted the show but not the Park.

Angry and frustrated, Roy returned to his suite at the Waldorf Astoria to consider his options. He'd been sure that either NBC or CBS would buy in — so sure, in fact, that he hadn't even made an appointment with ABC. In desperation, he called Leonard Goldenson, who had managed the restructuring of ABC after its merger with United Paramount Theaters. Goldenson came to Roy's hotel suite, studied the rendering, read the prospectus — then said, "Tell Walt he can have whatever he wants."

ABC put up $500,000 in cash and co-signed $4.5 million in loans for 34.5 percent ownership of Disneyland, plus a weekly hour-long TV show. Other owners included

Walt Disney Productions, Western Printing and Lithographing Company (publishers of Little Golden Books), and Walt himself, who owned a 17.2 percent share.

The ownership group had assembled $6 million in capital and loan guarantees — far less than the $17 million that would ultimately be needed. But when *Disneyland* premiered on ABC on October 27, 1954, months before opening day, Walt's Park looked like it was already a success. Corporate sponsors quickly lined up to invest. TV enabled Walt to finance his dream.

Walt shows Orange County officials his plans for Disneyland, December 1954. (Photo: Orange County Archives)

Breaking New Ground

Walt broke ground for Disneyland on July 16, 1954, on a tract of former orange and walnut groves. A team of landscapers from WED Enterprises marked hundreds of orange trees for removal, and marked a few others to be retained. Trees tagged with red ribbons were to be bull-dozed while trees with green ribbons were to be spared. Unfortunately, the bulldozer operator was colorblind and removed *all* the trees in that section.

Today, no original orange trees exist in the Park. For many years, one of the surviving orange trees grew near the bungalows of the Disneyland Hotel, but the tree died in 1999, around the time the bungalows were demolished to make room for Downtown Disney, the shopping and dining district that opened in 2001.

There is only one living tree that was on the property before Walt acquired the land — a Canary Island date palm. Walt's horticulturalist, Morgan "Bill" Evans, told the story of that tree:

> Planted in 1896 by an early rancher, it was a stalwart and revered resident of his front lawn, admired by three generations of children and adults. One member of the family was married beneath it. When the owner of the land sold his acreage to Walt Disney in 1954, he requested that this venerable palm be preserved. Walt was more than happy to oblige, but since the tree stood in the middle of Section C of the projected parking lot, he ordered that it be carefully "balled," lifted tenderly from its old home and trundled, all fifteen tons of it, to Adventureland.[7]

Today that ancient palm tree, The Dominguez Tree, stands guard over the Indiana Jones FastPass kiosk. It's the oldest living thing in Disneyland, and the only living reminder of the hundreds of trees that once shaded the property where Walt's Disneyland stands today.

The Dominguez Tree — planted in the 19th century, still thriving in the 21st century. (Photo: Bethany Williams)

In the early 1950s, Anaheim was a tiny community in a lightly populated agricultural region, Orange County, California. The pre-Disneyland economy of the region was based almost entirely on citrus crops, avocados, and crude oil.

The completion of the Santa Ana Freeway (now Interstate 5) in 1954, and the opening of Disneyland in 1955, dramatically transformed the region. Today, the once-sparsely populated Orange County is the sixth most populous county in the nation, and more populous than twenty-one entire states — thanks in no small part to Walt and Disneyland.

When Pat Williams and I wrote *How to Be Like Walt* in 2004, Art Linkletter told us about his first visit to the Disneyland site:

> One day in 1954, Walt called me and said, "Art, let me take you for a ride down to Orange County and I'll show you where I'm going to build Disneyland."
>
> I loved to hear Walt talk about his big plans, so we drove down with some researchers from the Stanford Research Institute. We drove and drove — we were miles from any population center. We finally got to a place where some bulldozers had cleared out an orange grove. It looked like a big field of dirt clods.
>
> "Well," Walt said, "this is it." He looked around and he could see it all in his imagination — the Disneyland Railroad, Main Street, the Sleeping Beauty Castle, Adventureland, Frontierland, all of it. I looked around and saw nothing but a cow pasture. I thought, *My poor deluded friend! He'll go broke!*

"Art," he said, "There's a fortune to be made here. If you buy up all the property around Disneyland, in a year or two it'll be worth twenty times what you paid for it."

I was too smart to get caught up in Walt's enthusiasm! I didn't buy any real estate around Disneyland—and by being so "smart," I passed up a chance to make millions![8]

The Anaheim city planners gave Disneyland a memorable street address: 1313 Harbor Boulevard. Any odd number could have been assigned to the 1300 block of Harbor Boulevard, from 1301 to 1399 — so why 1313? Some Disney historians believe Walt specifically asked for that address. Walt, who was not a superstitious man, might have found it amusing to defy fate by requesting a doubly "unlucky" number for Disneyland.

I subscribe to a different theory. Here's a clue: What's the thirteenth letter in the alphabet? M! Put two M's side by side and what Disney character do you think of? That's right, it all started with a mouse.

On Wednesday night, October 27, 1954, three months after breaking ground for Disneyland, Walt hosted the first episode of *Disneyland* on ABC. He became "Uncle Walt" to generations of Americans, and was welcomed into millions of American homes. Months before opening day, Walt was creating excitement about Disneyland.

My friend Peggy Matthews Rose grew up in Orange County when Walt was building the Park. "On Wednesday nights in 1954," she recalls, "our family gathered in front of the magic box in the living room and Walt would tell us about the wonderful kingdom he was building. Sometimes, we'd get in the car and drive down Harbor

Boulevard. My heart would flutter like Tinker Bell's wings as I spotted the turrets of the castle above the trees." (Peggy later portrayed Peter Pan as a cast member in Fantasyland.)

Animator Ward Kimball recalled Walt's relentless pursuit of perfection as he built his Park: "He walked over every inch of Disneyland, telling them to move a fence a little more to the left because you couldn't see the boat as it came 'round the corner. I'd be with him out there, and he'd say, 'The lake is too small. Maybe we should make it larger. Let's find out if we can move the train wreck over another fifty feet.' . . . [Everything] you see at Disneyland, Walt checked on."[9]

ABC publicity photo of Fess Parker as Davy Crockett in "Davy Crockett Goes to Congress," airing January 26, 1955, on the Disneyland *TV show.*

On December 15, 1954, a *Disneyland* episode, "Davy Crockett, Indian Fighter," touched off a nationwide craze for Davy Crockett merchandise. When Disneyland opened, Frontierland was the busiest land in the Park. Crockett-style coonskin caps became Disneyland's top-selling souvenirs, generating a $100 million bonanza (my brother and I brought home coonskin caps from our first Disneyland trip in 1957).

Walt knew the Disneyland blueprints by heart. He made sure that one of the first buildings completed was the Main Street Fire House, because his private apartment would be on the second floor. He moved in as soon as possible so he could watch his magic kingdom take shape.

He chose retired Navy admiral Joseph Fowler to oversee Disneyland's construction. Fowler had commanded the San Francisco Naval Yard during World War II, and was once appointed by President Truman to the job of cutting wasteful spending in the Pentagon. Admiral Fowler was known for his ability to solve "unsolvable" problems. Walt found the retired admiral supervising a tract home project in the San Francisco Bay area, and Fowler was eager for a more exciting challenge.

The challenges and problems Joe Fowler confronted began multiplying soon after he was hired. In Adventureland, the mechanical elephants, hippos, and crocodiles of the Jungle Cruise broke down due to abrasive particles in the water damaging the servomotors. In Frontierland, the first attempt to fill the Rivers of America failed — the sandy soil drank up all the water (good drainage is great for orange trees, bad for theme parks).

Construction costs spiraled. When Walt broke ground on July 16, 1954, the budget was $4.5 million. By September, it was $7 million. By November, $11 million. By opening day, expenditures topped $17 million.

Walt had set an ambitious goal, choosing July 17, 1955, as opening day. He had given himself a year and a day to build his dream — and the odds were against him.

Opening Day

As the day approached for Disneyland's grand opening, Walt asked Art Linkletter to host the live ABC television special. Linkletter recommended two co-hosts who could perform on live television without a script: Ronald Reagan and Robert Cummings.

The Saturday before Disneyland opened, asphalt workers, painters, and plumbers worked through the night, tripping over TV crews trying to set up equipment for Sunday's live broadcast. Walt spent much of that night in the *20,000 Leagues Under the Sea* walk-through exhibit in Tomorrowland, spray gun in hand, painting the backdrop behind the giant squid. With him was Imagineer Ken Anderson, who was trying to get the squid's mechanical arms to function. Finally, Walt and Ken decided to call it a day. The squid refused to cooperate. The *20,000 Leagues* exhibit would open a few days late.

Walt and Ken walked up Main Street and took a break, sitting on the curb near the Town Square. They were savoring the peace and quiet when an electrician ran up and said, "There's no power on the Toad ride! Somebody cut the wires!"

Anderson volunteered to fix the problem. When he reached Mr. Toad's Wild Ride, he found the power cables disconnected, not cut — a minor act of sabotage related to a union dispute. Anderson got the attraction up and running, then he sat down for a brief rest — and he promptly fell asleep. He slept behind the Toad attraction through Disneyland's opening day.

Walt, meanwhile, took a stroll down Main Street, giving his new kingdom the once-over. Then he wearily climbed the stairs to his apartment over the Fire House and fell into bed. For the next hour, he was repeatedly awakened by frantic phone calls from people needing a decision from the boss.

Finally, Walt took the phone off the hook and slept.

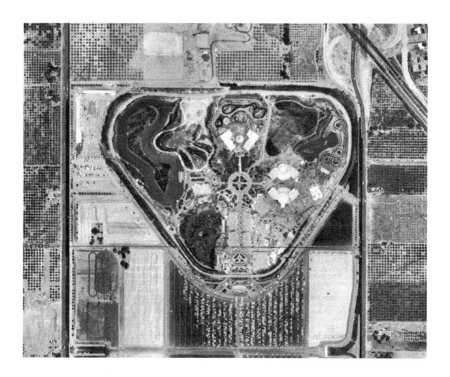

Aerial photo of Disneyland (surrounded by orange groves), taken July 15, 1955, just two days before opening day. (Photo: Orange County Archives)

After a few hours' sleep, Walt rose with the sun. He dressed and reviewed his mental checklist of the day's activities. Then, when he attempted to walk out of the apartment, he found the door wouldn't open. A worker had painted it shut from the other side. He was trapped. Walt phoned for a maintenance crew to rescue him.

After being freed, Walt headed for Town Square to meet with ABC personnel to discuss plans for the ninety-minute TV special, *Dateline: Disneyland*, which would air live from coast to coast at 4:30 p.m. Pacific time.

Only invited guests with VIP passes were supposed to attend on opening day. The Disney Company had issued 11,000 passes to studio employees, celebrities, and media outlets. But someone had sold thousands of forged passes on the black market — and more than *28,000 people* showed up. One enterprising miscreant with a folding ladder even charged five bucks a head to help people scale the back fence near Frontierland.

When the gates opened at ten a.m., Walt watched from his apartment, along with the Mouseketeers, whose ABC series *The Mickey Mouse Club* would premiere in October. Mouseketeer Sharon Baird later recalled:

> I was standing next to him at the window, watching the guests come pouring through the gates. When I looked up at him, he had his hands behind his back, a grin from ear to ear. I could see a lump in his throat and a tear streaming down his cheek. He had realized his dream. I was only twelve years old at the time, so it didn't mean as much to me then. But as the years go by, that image of him becomes more and more endearing.[10]

As opening day wore on, Walt's dream looked more and more like a nightmare: Hundred-plus degree heat. Too many guests, not enough restrooms, and not enough trash cans. Restaurants running out of food in the middle of lunchtime. Guests brushing up against wet paint or getting their shoes stuck in tarry asphalt on Main Street. Long lines at attractions, which malfunctioned at an alarming rate (the only ride that didn't break down at some point that day was The Jungle Cruise).

Restrooms ran out of supplies, and Walt was spotted carrying rolls of toilet paper to one of the men's rooms. Disneyland's streets were strewn with trash. Workers hauled load after load of garbage and piled it up behind the Main Street buildings. The Orange County Health Department later gave Walt an ultimatum: "This [trash] is either gone, or you're not open!"[11]

Disneyland designer Harper Goff was in the press room, trying to placate a hostile press corps. The reporters were accustomed to being plied with booze at grand openings and similar events — and there was no liquor in Disneyland. Goff told the angry mob of reporters that Walt wasn't legally permitted to serve alcohol on the premises.

The gentlemen of the press weren't interested in excuses. "Where's the nearest liquor store?" one reporter shouted. Goff said he didn't think there were any liquor stores in Anaheim.

An uprising ensued. Reporters threatened to make up negative stories and crucify Walt and his Park in the press — a threat that several reporters later carried out with vindictive glee.[12]

Walt was unaware of the problems. He was focused on his live television broadcast to ninety million viewers. Ronald Reagan hosted the dedication ceremony at Town Square where Walt, standing beside Governor Goodwin Knight of California, read the dedication plaque:

• Disneyland •

To all who come to this happy place,
Welcome.

Disneyland is your land. Here
age relives fond memories of the past,
and here youth may savor the challenge
and promise of the future.

Disneyland is dedicated to the
ideals, the dreams, and the hard facts
which have created America, with
the hope that it will be a source of joy
and inspiration to all the world.

July 17, 1955

As the American flag was hoisted over Town Square, the United States Marine Band played "The Star-Spangled Banner" and a jet squadron from the California National Guard flew over the Park. Walt and the governor climbed into a 1903 Pierce automobile and led the first Disneyland parade down Main Street toward the Castle, followed by floats and stagecoaches with Disney stars and characters.

Throughout the broadcast, ABC cameras located Hollywood stars enjoying their first day at Disneyland: Frank Sinatra and Sammy Davis, Jr., racing on the Autopia, Danny Thomas with his family in Tomorrowland, Irene Dunne christening the *Mark Twain*, Alan Young emerging from Peter Pan's Flight, and Jerry Colonna (the voice of the March Hare in *Alice in Wonderland*) at the throttle of the Casey Jr. Circus Train. In Frontierland, Fess Parker and Buddy Ebsen performed a medley of songs from *Davy Crockett*.

The Dedication Plaque Walt read on July 17, 1955,
located at the base of the flagpole in Town Square.

During a commercial break, Walt hurried to his next camera location — but was stopped by a security guard who said, "You can't go through there."

"Do you know who I am?"

"Yes, Mr. Disney, but I have my orders."

"Mister, if you don't get out of my way, I'll walk right over the top of you!"

The guard stepped aside.

Despite minor miscues, the broadcast went smoothly, showing off the attractions, the railroad, and the iconic Sleeping Beauty Castle. The TV cameras caught thousands of children and grownups smiling, laughing, and enjoying the realization of Walt's vision.

Media cynics scorned Disneyland, betting it would fail. One newspaper denounced Disneyland as "The $17 Million People Trap That Mickey Mouse Built."[13] But

Walt's vision outlasted the cynics and proved them wrong. Attendance during Disneyland's first year topped 3.6 million people. These days, the Park welcomes about 16 million guests per year.

Disneyland opened to the public on Monday, July 18. Price of admission: one dollar. Inside the Park, guests purchased attraction tickets on a pay-per-ride basis. Though admission was inexpensive, guests shelled out cash all day long. By October, Disney offered "Value Books" with A, B, and C coupons worth 10, 20, and 30 cents. D coupons worth 35 cents were introduced in 1956, and E coupons worth 50 cents appeared in June 1959. The Value Book coupons and ticket booths were discontinued in mid-1982, replaced by a system of higher main gate admission prices along with free rides and shows throughout the Park.

Credit cards would not be invented until three years after the Park opened, so Disneyland was an all-cash business in those early days. There were no automated coin counters and sorters, yet so much cash sloshed through Disneyland that the company had to invent new ways to count it. At the main gate and ticket booths, clerks dumped loose bills and change into metal fire buckets by their feet. Runners collected the buckets from the booths and carried them to the office behind City Hall. There, paper money was counted and coins were weighed — so many pounds of quarters equals so many dollars, and so forth.

Disneyland got a huge boost when *The Mickey Mouse Club* premiered on ABC, October 3, 1955. At 5 p.m. every weeknight, three-fourths of American TV sets were tuned to the Mouseketeers. Host Jimmy Dodd was a Disney songwriter. Co-host Roy "Moose" Williams had been a Disney artist since 1929. Nicknamed "The Big Moose-keteer," Roy often drew Disney characters on-camera.

Roy Williams was often in the Park, drawing souvenir cartoons for guests. (Photo: Peggy Matthews Rose)

"Moose" Williams' most important contribution was his design of the Mickey Mouse ears worn by the Mouse-keteers. In a 1929 Mickey Mouse short, *The Karnival Kid*, Roy animated Mickey tipping his "hat" (his mouse ears) to Minnie. Roy revived the idea when he helped design the Mouseketeers' costumes. During the network run of *The Mickey Mouse Club*, Disneyland sold up to 20,000 Mickey Mouse hats per day.

In 1960, the Disney Company bought back the ABC network's 34.5 percent stake in Disneyland. The network realized a $7.5 million return on a $500,000 investment.

Walt continued to walk around his Park, wait in the lines, ride the attractions with his guests, and listen to their comments. He encouraged his Imagineers to ride the rides and eat their meals in the Park. He was continually seeking to improve the Disneyland experience.

Though Disneyland has changed since Walt passed away, much of Walt's original Disneyland is still on display. His ideas still entertain and inspire us.

Walt Disney lives on in his Park. Come with me. Let's go find him.

CHAPTER THREE

Walt's Main Street USA

"For those of us who remember the carefree time it re-creates, Main Street will bring back happy memories. For younger visitors, it is an adventure in turning back the calendar to the days of their grandfather's youth."
—*Walt Disney*

There's a story often told about Walt, though I've never been able to confirm it: Walt was walking through Tomorrowland when he came upon a jarring sight — a cowboy from Frontierland walking by in full costume, wearing a Stetson hat, six shooters, boots, and jingling spurs. Clearly, cowboys from yesteryear have no place in Tomorrowland.

So Walt made it clear to the cowboy that he was to go backstage and change out of costume before leaving Frontierland. Whether this incident happened or not, the story makes an important point: If you go to Disneyland, you'll never see a cowboy in Tomorrowland. Why? Because Disneyland is more than a theme park. Disneyland is a *show* — and you, Walt's guest, are both the star and the audience. Walt made sure you would never find a single false detail to spoil the illusion.

The experience begins as you approach Disneyland from the esplanade. Towering behind the turnstiles like a cinema marquee is the Main Street Train Station with its clock tower and a sign announcing, "DISNEYLAND — Population 650,000,000 — Elevation 138 Feet."

Main Street Train Station and Mickey floral display.

You pass through the turnstile and into Disneyland's forecourt, and there's the Mickey Mouse floral display. Mickey is Walt's alter ego and trademark, like the studio logo at the beginning of a movie. The floral display declares that Disneyland is "A Walt Disney Production." It consists of more than 30,000 individual plants which are changed eight times a year. It has been a part of Disneyland since opening day.

Next, notice the red brick pavement. The forecourt is Walt's red carpet, welcoming you to the movie experience of your choice. You are the celebrity. Choose your own adventure. Past, future, or realms of imagination — where do you want to go today?

The first choice to make: Left or right? Two tunnels lead under the railroad tracks. Posters on the tunnel walls announce "coming attractions" in Tomorrowland, Fantasyland, Frontierland, and Adventureland.

Emerging from the tunnel, you see what the motion picture trade calls an "establishing shot" — a wide shot that tells you the time and setting you're entering. Stepping out of the right-hand tunnel, you see the Town Square, the Disney Gallery, and the Main Street Opera House. From the left-hand tunnel, you see the City Hall, the Fire House, and The Emporium. Your immersion in Walt's "movie" is subliminally reinforced by the aroma of buttered popcorn from a nearby vending cart.

You've just entered another time, another reality: Main Street USA, circa 1910, the idealized hometown of Walt's childhood.

The Music and Spirit of Main Street

Like most movies, Disneyland has a soundtrack. You may not notice the music at first, but you'll find a bounce in your step and a smile on your face as you walk to the strains of "Oh You Beautiful Doll," "Meet Me in St. Louis, Louis," "In the Good Old Summer Time," "The Maple Leaf Rag," and "Dearie."

You'll hear Broadway hits like "Gary, Indiana," from *The Music Man*, "Surrey with the Fringe on Top" from *Oklahoma!*, and "Put on Your Sunday Clothes" from *Hello Dolly!* (reprised in the Disney/Pixar film *WALL·E*). From Disney's *Summer Magic*, you'll hear "Flitterin'," and "Beautiful Beulah." From *The Happiest Millionaire*, you'll hear "Fortuosity" and "Let's Have a Drink on It."

The music is perfectly suited to the opening scenes of Walt's Main Street show. The soundtrack prepares you for a day in the Happiest Place on Earth. But before the music moves you down Main Street, you may want to pause at the Guest Relations kiosk to pick up a Celebration Button. Over the years, Disneyland has offered free buttons for many occasions — Happy Birthday, Just Married, First Visit, Happy Anniversary, and more.

One of the nostalgic features of Main Street USA is the resident barbershop quartet, the Dapper Dans. Since 1959, the Dans have performed everything from popular standards to Disney classics in the barbershop style. They sometimes sing while cycling on a custom-made Schwinn four-seater commissioned by Walt himself.

If you want to experience Walt's *original* Disneyland, Star Tours and Indiana Jones can wait. Slow down and enjoy the sounds of America's past.

The Town Square, Opera House, City Hall, and Fire House

The Town Square is the cultural and municipal district of Main Street USA. The cultural district is on the east side of the Square — the Opera House (the oldest building in Disneyland) and the Disney Gallery (which was the Bank of America branch from 1955 to 1993).

The Opera House was originally closed to the public. From 1955 to 1961, it was Disneyland's carpentry shop. Much of the decorative woodwork around the Park was created there. From 1961 to 1963, the Opera House hosted the *Babes in Toyland* exhibit, honoring the 1961 musical starring Ray Bolger and Annette Funicello.

In 1960, Walt committed his company, WED Enterprises, to creating an exhibit for the 1964 World's Fair to honor Abraham Lincoln. Walt's Imagineers had just invented a new technology for The Enchanted Tiki Room in Adventureland. They called it Audio-Animatronics, and they used this new technology to create a lifelike version of the sixteenth president. After a successful run at the World's Fair, Great Moments with Mr. Lincoln premiered at the Opera House on Disneyland's tenth anniversary, July 17, 1965.

The municipal district of Main Street is on the west side of the Town Square — City Hall and the Fire House. Designed by Harper Goff, City Hall was inspired by the courthouse of Goff's hometown of Fort Collins, Colorado, and serves as Disneyland's guest relations center. There you'll find answers to questions, pick up maps and event schedules, obtain special assistance passes for people with disabilities, and more. There's also a wall map of Disneyland in braille.

At City Hall, birthday boys and birthday girls can speak by phone with Disney characters, get autographed character photos, and obtain birthday buttons. Children with birthday buttons receive greetings, stickers, and other freebies from cast members throughout the day.

Disneyland visitors are often in such a hurry to get to their favorite attraction that they rush past the Fire House next to City Hall. At the Fire House, you'll experience Walt's love of the past. Take note of the fire-fighting equipment and historic photos on the walls.

Inspect the horse-drawn fire wagon parked there. When Disneyland opened in 1955, guests could ride down Main Street on the fire wagon. It was pulled by two horses, Bess and Jess, whose stalls now stand empty. The fire wagon was retired and put on display in 1960.

Notice also the brass fireman's pole. The second floor of the Fire House was Walt's private apartment, where he lived during construction of the Park, and where he spent many days and nights after the Park opened. The pole connected Walt's private apartment with the Fire House below. Some say that Walt was so eager to start his day at Disneyland that he'd slide down the pole and exit through the Fire House onto Main Street.

Walt's daughter, Diane Disney Miller, was asked if her father ever slid down the pole. Her reply: "I'm sure he didn't."[1] But she recalled a time Walt invited others to use the pole.

"There was some event [at Disneyland] that day," she said, "and Fess Parker and Buddy Ebsen [the stars of the *Davy Crockett* series on *Disneyland*] were both out there for it, and Dad was looking out that window and saw them and he said, 'Hey, come on up!' "

So Fess and Buddy went up to the apartment and, at Walt's invitation, slid down the pole.[2]

According to legend, a visitor once shinnied up the pole from inside the Fire House while the Disney family was in the apartment upstairs. Disneyland management sealed the hole in the Fire House ceiling to prevent a recurrence — or so the legend claims. However, the upper end of the pole is inside a closet, behind a closed door. An intruder couldn't simply climb the pole and poke his head up into Walt's apartment. I suspect the intruder legend is untrue.

Walt's apartment was decorated in elegant Victorian style by Hollywood set decorator Emile Kuri, who had worked on many period films, including *20,000 Leagues Under the Sea*. In addition to the cranberry glass lamps, grandfather clock, and other period pieces, the apartment contains many curios that Walt and Lillian Disney picked up on their travels.

When Walt was in the Park, he would light a lamp in the apartment window to let his staff know he was on the property. Ever since Walt's death, that lamp has remained lit as a tribute to Disneyland's late founder — except at Christmastime, when it is replaced by a lighted Christmas tree.

For years after Walt's death, his apartment was treated like a shrine. It was kept locked and unused but meticulously maintained. There are still utensils and appliances in the kitchenette that Walt used to make his own lunch.

Peggy Matthews Rose recalls, "When I worked in the Disney University from 1976 to 1980, we all thought of Walt's apartment as holy ground. No one I knew had ever been in the apartment, so the closest we could get to being there was an article in the August 1963 *National Geographic* that profiled the Disney family and showcased the apartment.

"About twenty years later, when I was working with the merchandise division, Disney's CEO at the time, Michael Eisner, decided to open the apartment exclusively for company use. I was assigned to facilitate small group forums in the apartment, so I got to go up early to open Walt's apartment, let the catering people in, and air out the place. As you can imagine, it was a bit musty after three decades of being largely unused.

"This was where the Disney family had gathered in the 1950s and '60s. From that window, Walt watched Disneyland being built. And from that window, he saw the first crowds streaming into the Park on opening day. Being in that apartment stirs your emotions. You feel close to Walt there."

On opening day in 1955, a Dixieland jazz band, the Firehouse Five Plus Two, performed at the Fire House, perched on the fire engine in full regalia. Formed in the 1940s, the band consisted largely of Disney artists. Ward Kimball was the bandleader, sound effects man, and trombonist. Animator Frank Thomas played the piano, Harper Goff strummed the banjo, story man Ed Penner played tuba, and animator Clarke Mallery played clarinet. Cornet player Danny Alguire and drummer Monte Mountjoy were professional musicians who had previously played with the Texas Playboys.

Kimball recalled, "Walt told us to wander around the Park and play wherever there was a crowd. We were the first mobile band at Disneyland."[3]

The centerpiece of the Town Square is a triangular-shaped park, which is much as Walt envisioned it in his 1948 memo about a place he called Mickey Mouse Park: "The Main Village, which includes the Railroad Station, is built around a village green."

A bandstand once stood on the green. Before the Park opened, Walt realized it blocked the view across the Town Square. He had the bandstand moved near the Central Plaza for a while, then to Adventureland near the Jungle Cruise. In 1962, when the Jungle Cruise was expanded to include the elephant bathing pool, Walt donated the bandstand to the city of Anaheim. It now stands in Rogers Gardens, a botanical nursery in Corona Del Mar.

On the east and west sides of the village green are two nineteenth century cannons. They were once owned by the French army, but were never fired in battle. The cannons were forged by the French arms manufacturer Hotchkiss et Cie, founded in Saint-Denis by American gunsmith Benjamin B. Hotchkiss.

The elaborate black base of the Disneyland flagpole once supported a street light on Wilshire Boulevard in Los Angeles. Disneyland designer Emile Kuri was driving along Wilshire when he passed an automobile accident. A car had knocked down a street light pole, but the base was undamaged. Kuri bought the entire pole for five dollars and used the decorative base to anchor the sixty-five-foot flagpole.

At around 4:30 every afternoon, Disneyland conducts a Flag Retreat ceremony on the green. The Disneyland Band plays and the Dapper Dans sing "You're a Grand Old Flag" and "America the Beautiful." The Band also plays the official songs of each branch of military service as members of the military are invited to stand around the flagpole to be publicly honored. Then, as the Disneyland Band plays the National Anthem, the flag is reverently lowered and precisely folded. The entire ceremony usually lasts about twenty minutes.

This patriotic display is about as "Walt-ish" as it gets. He once said, "I get red, white, and blue at times." Walt always watched the flag-raising and flag-lowering ceremonies from his apartment window whenever he was in the Park.

In the fall, Disneyland dresses up the village green with a sixteen-foot-tall Mickey Mouse jack-o'-lantern.

At Christmastime, the green features an elaborately-trimmed sixty-foot Christmas tree, and Main Street is decked in wreaths, lights, and ornaments.

The gas-fired streetlamps along Main Street are well over a hundred years old, and once illuminated the streets of Baltimore, Maryland. Disneyland bought them as scrap metal for three cents a pound.

Walt's Shopping District

Walt's brother Roy once said, "Main Street has the nostalgic quality that makes it everybody's hometown. It is Main Street USA. Three blocks long, it is the main shopping district of Disneyland. It has a bank and a newspaper office, and the little ice cream parlor with the marble-topped tables and wire-backed chairs. There is a penny arcade and nickelodeon where you can see old-time movies. On the corner is the great Disneyland Emporium where you can buy almost anything and everything unusual."[4]

Main Street USA has changed very little since Walt unveiled it on July 17, 1955. Five Main Street attractions and shops have been there since opening day — City Hall, the Fire House, The Emporium, The Penny Arcade, and the Main Street Cinema. Take a moment to enjoy the animated dioramas in the Emporium's windows. Or linger in the Arcade and listen to the restored 1907 Welte Orchestrion self-playing pipe organ that Walt himself purchased in 1953.

The Candy Palace opened July 22, 1955, and continues to grace Main Street with its nostalgic fragrances (vanilla most of the year, peppermint and gingerbread at Christmastime). The scents come from a device called a

Smellitzer (a portmanteau of "smell" and "howitzer"). Other shops dating to Walt's era include the Magic Shop and the 20th Century Music Company.

The shop called The China Closet began on opening day as Ruggles China & Gifts, an independently owned shop that rented space in Disneyland. The original proprietors, Phil and Sophie Papel, named the store after character actor Charles Ruggles, who starred in the 1932 Paramount film *If I Had a Million.*

Ruggles China & Gifts sold exquisite imported crystal and ceramicware, plus inexpensive grab bags of beautiful items the Papels picked up at closeouts. Phil and Sophie Papel warehoused their merchandise in a farmhouse in nearby Garden Grove. Their thirteen-year-old son and eight-year-old daughter helped out in the store.

Merchants like the Papels helped ensure the early success of Disneyland. Walt was a filmmaker, and knew little about the retail business. So he invited merchants to set up shop on Main Street USA. Out of money, his credit line exhausted, Walt relied on both big corporations and small mom-and-pop shops to finance his Park.

Walt required merchants to pay for the Victorian-era decor and antique fixtures in their shops — an expensive proposition that included a lot of beveled glass, carved wood, brass fittings, and velvet curtains. Merchants also paid their entire first year's lease in advance.

In the early 1960s, Disneyland exercised its option to take over several Main Street stores, including Ruggles China & Gifts. Disney historian Dave Mason notes that Walt made sure that Phil and Sophie Papel "were treated fairly during this transition, and as a result, the Papel family has a deep appreciation for both Walt Disney and for their own contributions to the continuing success of

Disneyland." Their Main Street store helped launch their twenty-store retail chain and wholesale business.[5]

The Small Town Experience

Main Street USA is the Main Street of Walt's boyhood memories. Today, there are six Disney theme parks around the world — Anaheim, Orlando, Tokyo, Paris, Hong Kong, and Shanghai — but Anaheim's Main Street USA is the only one Walt personally oversaw. The others are different in scale and detail from Walt's original vision. (Shanghai Disneyland, in fact, replaced Main Street with Mickey Avenue, inspired by Disney cartoon characters.) Only in Disneyland can you experience *Walt's* Main Street USA.

The Main Streets in other Disney parks are broader and the shops more spacious, but Disneyland's Main Street is more intimate. The smaller scale of Disneyland gives Main Street USA a more convincing "small town" feel, as Walt intended.

Walt designed Disneyland to impact our senses in very specific ways. His philosophy of theme park design involves something he called a "wienie." Walt loved hot dogs. He ate them cold right out of the refrigerator, and he used them to teach his dog Lady to perform tricks. Walt realized he could use tall, highly visible structures, which he called "wienies," to draw crowds in a desired direction.

"Wienies" tower above the trees, catch the eye, and subliminally whisper, "Come this way." The grandest "wienie" in Disneyland is Sleeping Beauty Castle. Walt wanted the Castle to be tall enough that people could orient themselves from anyplace in the Park. Other Disneyland "wienies" from Walt's era include:

- The Main Street Train Station, which drew visitors from the parking lot toward the main gate;

- The *Mark Twain* Riverboat, with its twin smokestacks, drawing guests to Frontierland;

- The 147-foot-tall Matterhorn, the tallest attraction in the Park;

- The Moonliner; Walt's seventy-six-foot-tall spaceship attracted crowds to Tomorrowland from 1955 until its demise in 1967;

- The Chicken of the Sea Pirate Ship; with its red-and-white sails and high golden stern, this ship-shape restaurant beckoned crowds from opening day until its demolition in 1982.

These days, Disney officials avoid the term "wienie." Disney historian Jim Korkis says that when he worked at Disney Institute, he was told to substitute "carrot" or "visual magnet" in place of Walt's word.

Yet Walt would never have dangled a "carrot" before his guests. His term "wienie," however inelegant, was deliberate. A "wienie," to Walt, was a *treat*. Korkis explains, "Walt claimed he never controlled people, but that he controlled the experience and that resulted in the guests making the right choices."[6]

Go to Main Street and see for yourself how Walt controlled the experience. Sleeping Beauty Castle attracts the crowd so that Main Street doesn't become congested. But you can only see the Castle if you walk down the middle of the street. If you're on the sidewalk, trees hide the Castle. Walt knew exactly what he was doing.

People walking down the middle of Main Street are in a hurry to get to other attractions — and the Castle draws them along, as Walt intended. But Walt hid the Castle from those who want to take their time and do some window shopping. He placed store windows low enough that children could look in. Walt wanted each guest to choose the pace, direction, and destination of his or her own adventure.

Walt originally planned to have side streets branching off from Main Street, giving his guests more pathways to explore. As late as 1959, official maps of Disneyland showed a side street just past the Opera House, which would have led to Liberty Street, a celebration of America's founding. At the end of Main Street, around the corner and to the right, early maps showed a street leading to Edison Square, celebrating the history of electricity. Though never built, these attractions demonstrate Walt's vision of Disneyland as a place to be explored and discovered.

Disneyland's walkways never intersect at right angles. They meander to gently unfold their charm. As you head toward the Castle, there's a little side street just past the Market House on your right, and another just past the Fortuosity Shop on your left (the Fortuosity Shop was the Upjohn Pharmacy in Walt's era). Enter these alleyways and you'll hear the voices of make-believe citizens of Main Street. From upper story windows come sounds of a dentist drilling, a man singing in the shower, and a child taking a piano lesson.

Main Street USA is a different experience at different times of the day. In the evening, as dusk settles, crowds throng the street, waiting for the final parade of the day and the nightly fireworks show. After the fireworks, there's a mass exodus that chokes Main Street — but don't get caught in the crowd. Instead, duck into a store and browse for, oh, half an hour or so.

When you step back outside, the street will be practically empty. You'll hear music playing. The vibe will be calm, unhurried. You'll almost feel you *own* Disneyland — and you'll know how Walt must have felt as he strolled the quiet streets of his kingdom after closing.

Examine the architecture of Main Street — the rooflines defined by thousands of lights, echoing Walt's memories of Electric Park. Notice the windows, gables, and gingerbread of the façades. Walt's designers have crafted a mood out of light and shadow. Just as Main Street in the daytime fills the senses with color and sound, Main Street at night fills the soul with quiet nostalgia.

The Main Street Windows

In Walt's Disneyland "motion picture," the upper story windows along Main Street serve as the opening credits — or, if you are leaving, the closing credits. These are the names of the artists, Imagineers, and inventors who helped build Disneyland. The windows often involve an in-joke related to that person's hobby or expertise.

For example, a window above the Opera House reads, "Milt Albright — Entrepreneur — No Job Too Big — No Job Too Small." Albright managed various operations in the early years of the Park.

Longtime art director and Imagineer Ken Anderson, has a window above the Market House that reads, "Ken Anderson — Bait Co." (Ironically, Anderson — an avid catch-and-release fly fisherman — didn't use bait.)

A window above the Carnation Café reads, "Golden Vaudeville Routines — Wally Boag — Prop." Boag played Pecos Bill in the long-running Golden Horseshoe Revue in Frontierland. "Prop" is not only short for "proprietor" but a pun on the props he famously used in his comedy act, such as the countless broken teeth (actually, navy beans) he spit out when knocked in the mouth, and his "Boag-alloon" balloon animals.

Roger E. Broggie, the original Disney Imagineer, is honored with a window above the Main Street Magic Shop: " 'Can Do' Machine Works — Mechanical Wonders — Live Steam Engines — Magical Illusions — Cameras — Roger Broggie, Shopmaster — 'Adviser to the Magic Makers.' "

One window honors Ron Dominguez, whose family owned an orange grove on the Disneyland site. He was born in a house where Pirates of the Caribbean stands today. Hired as a cast member before the Park opened, Dominguez rose to become head of Disneyland attractions. His window over the Market House reads, "Orange Grove Property Mgt. – 'We Care For Your Property As If It Were Our Own' — Ron Dominguez — Owner."

Elias Disney's window at the Emporium (photo: HarshLight)[7]; and Walt's window next to the Main Street Cinema.

For Disneyland's fiftieth anniversary, a first-story window was unveiled on the Main Street Cinema door, honoring Walt himself and all Disneyland cast members. It reads, "Open Since '55 — Disneyland Casting Agency — 'It takes People to Make the Dream a Reality' — Walter Elias Disney, Founder & Director Emeritus."

Walt memorialized his father with this window above the Emporium: "Elias Disney — Contractor — Est. 1895." The more you know about Disneyland and the people who built it, the more meaningful those windows become.

Many Disneyland shops and attractions have come and gone. The Bank of America had a full-service branch next to the Opera House from 1955 to 1993. The Story Book Shop, operated by Western Printing and Lithographing Company (publisher of Little Golden Books) was a Main Street fixture from 1955 to 1995. The Main Street Shooting Gallery was open from 1955 to 1962. The Wurlitzer Music Hall occupied the corner across the street from the Emporium from 1955 to 1968.

From 1955 to 1990, Main Street had a cigar shop called Fine Tobacco, between the Magic Shop and the Main Street Cinema. It sold cigars, cigarettes, pipes, and loose tobacco, and gave away free matchbooks. The cigar shop is gone, but the wooden Indian that stood outside remains.

One shop you'd probably *not* expect in Disneyland is a place to buy bras, lingerie, and torsolettes. But when Disneyland opened in 1955, there stood the Intimate Apparel Shop, presented by the Hollywood-Maxwell Brassiere Compay of Los Angeles. Not only could you purchase unmentionables there, but you could learn the immodest history of underthings in the shop's modest museum.

The shop's genial host was "The Wizard of Bras," a mechanical figure that gave a recorded lecture on underwear. Some Disney historians say "The Wizard of Bras" was the earliest Disneyland robot, though it wasn't as sophisticated as later Audio-Animatronic figures.

The Intimate Apparel Shop was on the east side of the street, just beyond the Silhouette Studio. While all the other shops on Main Street fronted against the "build-to line," the Victorian façade of the Intimate Apparel Shop was set back from the street. It was the only shop on Main Street with a front porch.

The shop closed in January 1956 after six months in operation. The door was sealed in 1959, and is now locked and unmarked. The space the shop once occupied is now part of the China Closet next door. The porch still offers a bench and two chairs where you can sit and watch people go by.

Above the former shop is a window honoring Imagineer Roland Fargo "Rolly" Crump, who helped create the Enchanted Tiki Room, The Haunted Mansion, and "it's a small world."[8] The window reads, "Fargo's Palm Parlor — Predictions That Will Haunt You — Bazaar, Whimsical & Weird — Designs to Die For — Roland F. Crump — Assistant to the Palm Reader." (The word "Bazaar" is a deliberate pun, not a typo; it refers to Rolly's work on the Adventureland Bazaar.)

Continuing on toward the Castle, there's an oddity known as the "Test Wall" at the end of Center Street, which branches off to the right just past the Market House. It was probably used to demonstrate different styles and patterns of brick to Walt as Disneyland was under construction. The wall is tucked away to the right of the guest lockers. A drinking fountain is set into the middle of the wall.

The Test Wall is made of mismatched bricks — a glaring imperfection in Walt's otherwise-perfect Main Street USA. It has been there since 1955, and no one knows why it was never renovated. Did Walt forget it was there? Possibly. It's in an out-of-the-way place that Walt might have never visited after the Park opened. Perhaps the Test Wall had simply been forgotten — even by Walt.

After you check out the Test Wall, stop at the Market House for a cup of coffee. Notice the old-fashioned phones — a Market House fixture since 1955. Pick up the phone and you can eavesdrop on a "party line" conversation straight from the early 1900s.

The Psychology of Scale

As Margaret J. King and J. G. O'Boyle observed in *Disneyland and Culture*, Walt's Park doesn't offer reality, but *hyperreality* — "a tightly edited, stylized, and focused version of reality, shaped to advance a specific narrative." The Park uses a technology of "altered scale, re-engineered perspective, color, harmonics, texture, lighting, sound, and iconography, all combined to produce an effect 'more real than real.'"

King and O'Boyle note that Main Street speaks to us through the thematic language of the senses: "the town square, the music of a brass band, the clang of a trolley bell, the hiss of steam from the wood-burning locomotive, the American flag flying above gabled rooftops, the gingerbread detailing on the shopfronts." These impressions subconsciously anchor us in a gentler, simpler time and place — the small-town America of Walt's boyhood.

After Walt Disney's death, the Disney Company, led by Walt's brother Roy, built a second and much larger version of Disneyland — the Magic Kingdom at Walt Disney World in Florida. King and O'Boyle observe that when people have visited both Disneyland and the Magic Kingdom, "the almost universal preference" is for Disneyland.

Why do people prefer the original Anaheim park, with its narrower streets and plazas, its reduced-scale buildings, and its smaller Castle? After all, Florida's Cinderella Castle is almost two and a half times the height of Disneyland's Sleeping Beauty Castle. Isn't bigger better?

There are reasons people might prefer Walt's smaller Disneyland over Florida's Magic Kingdom. For example, Disneyland is less spread out, and hence less tiring to walk through. Also, Disneyland was conceived, designed, and built by Walt himself. As Peggy Matthews Rose pointed out to me, Disneyland is the only Disney theme park that *literally* has Walt's fingerprints on it.

But King and O'Boyle suggest a subtle and subliminal reason: The reduced scale of Anaheim's Disneyland "replicates the feeling of returning to childhood haunts as an adult when 'everything looks so much smaller.' The full-scale Walt Disney World Main Street, set along a broader avenue, is less successful in evoking welcoming 'childhood' memories."[9]

Had Walt lived to build the Magic Kingdom in Florida, would he have built it on such a large scale? Perhaps not.

As a filmmaker, Walt had an intuitive grasp of the subliminal effect of scale on the human consciousness. Most
movie sets are built at a slightly reduced scale in order
to psychologically increase the stature of the actors and
the characters they portray. Walt used this same effect
of reduced scale to enable the "actors" in his Disneyland
"movie" — his guests — to see themselves as larger than
their surroundings and more in control.

Many people believe Disneyland was built entirely at
a five-eighths scale. This is not strictly true. Different
scales are used in different parts of the Park. The buildings of Main Street USA use forced perspective to make
them seem taller than they are. The ground floor is built
at seven-eighths scale, the second story at five-eighths
scale, and the third story at one-half scale. This means
that everything you see — bricks, doors, windows, lamps
— are made to the scale for that particular level.

Walt understood that post-WWII Americans felt lost
in a world of towering skyscrapers, troubling global
events, and increasing depersonalization. He created
Main Street USA not only as a place of nostalgia, but as
a place of small-town values and small-town scale. You
won't feel diminished or unimportant in Walt's Disneyland. There are no skyscrapers here.

The Central Plaza (or Hub)

Between the end of Main Street and the drawbridge of
Sleeping Beauty Castle lies a circular plaza. It is officially called the Central Plaza, but Walt called it "the
Hub" because it reminded him of the hub of a wagon
wheel. Accordingly, Disneyland cast members have been
calling it the Hub for decades.

Here Main Street vehicles circle around for their return trip to Town Square. And here the pathways radiate like wagon wheel spokes to the four original lands of Walt's Disneyland — Adventureland, Frontierland, Fantasyland, and Tomorrowland. In Walt's day, the Plaza was a miniature park with trees, flowers, and umbrella-shaded benches, plus a red turn-of-the-century popcorn wagon.

"Partners" by Blaine Gibson.
(Photo: Christopher Wood / wood26)[10]

On November 18, 1993, sixty-five years after the premiere of *Steamboat Willie*, Walt's nephew, Roy E. Disney, unveiled a bronze statue in the center of the Plaza — "Partners," sculpted by Imagineer Blaine Gibson. The statue depicts Walt hand-in-hand with Mickey Mouse.

With his right hand, Walt points toward the horizon, as if to say, "Look at what we built together."

Blaine Gibson had worked for Walt since the 1940s and knew Walt well. He not only captured the look of joy in Walt's eyes, but he also included two fine details: the STR emblem on Walt's tie (referring to Smoke Tree Ranch, near Palm Springs, where Walt had a vacation home); and the Irish Claddagh wedding ring on his right hand. (Walt bought matching Claddagh rings for himself and Lillian during a 1948 vacation in Ireland).[11]

The statue was rededicated on December 5, 2001, Walt's hundredth birthday. During the ceremony, Disney songwriter Richard Sherman performed Walt's favorite song, "Feed the Birds," from *Mary Poppins*. As Sherman began singing, "Tuppence, tuppence, tuppence a bag," a white bird swooped low over Sherman's piano, then soared away. Sherman took it as a sign that Walt was watching — and he approved.

The spirit of Walt Disney does seem to hover over Disneyland. During the last eleven years of his life, people often found him in the Park, sitting on a bench or talking with his guests, experiencing his magical kingdom through their eyes. In Main Street, more than any other part of Disneyland, you and I can rediscover Disneyland as Walt envisioned it — and loved it.

CHAPTER FOUR

Walt's Railroad and Vehicles

"I just want [Disneyland] to look like nothing else in the world. And it should be surrounded by a train."
—Walt Disney

Disney animator (and steam train enthusiast) Ward Kimball picked up the phone and heard, "Ward, this is Walt."

"Walt who?"

"Walt Disney, for crying out loud! How would you like to go with me to the Railroad Fair in Chicago?"

"When do we leave?"

On Sunday, July 18, 1948, Walt and Ward boarded the Super Chief at Pasadena station. In the past, Walt had rarely opened up about his life to others. Though Kimball had worked for Walt since 1934, he had never known much about Walt's early years. But during the forty-hour train ride, the two men talked endlessly.

Walt told Kimball stories from his childhood, his time as an ambulance driver in France, and the painful experience of being cheated out of his creation, Oswald the Lucky Rabbit. Kimball later said, "Much of what he told me, I'd never heard before."

The Railroad Fair opened on Tuesday, July 20, and the two men stayed for four days. There were hundreds of trains on display, from nineteenth-century steam locomotives to the sleek stainless steel *Zephyr*. The two men talked to scores of railroad engineers, firemen, and brakemen. They walked through vintage railroad cars and climbed into the cabs of antique steam locomotives. At night, they watched the fireworks reflecting off Lake Michigan.

A replica of President Lincoln's funeral train rolled slowly down the tracks while a brass band played "The Battle Hymn of the Republic." Walt, who had always felt a spiritual bond with Lincoln, was moved to tears. The experience may have partially inspired Great Moments with Mr. Lincoln, which Walt unveiled at the Main Street Opera House, July 18, 1965.

From the Railroad Fair in Chicago, Walt and Ward took the Wabash Railway to Dearborn, Michigan, to visit the Henry Ford Museum and Greenfield Village. Ford had purchased entire buildings from across the country to put on display — the Illinois courthouse where Lincoln practiced law; the Wright Brothers' Dayton, Ohio, bicycle shop; Noah Webster's Connecticut home; and Henry Ford's birthplace and the garage where he built his first car.

Greenfield Village also featured a nostalgic transportation system that included a horse-drawn omnibus, working Ford Model T's, and The Edison, an 1870s-style steam-powered train. A double-decker sternwheeler, the *Suwanee*, made a circuit around a loop in the Rouge River, just as Walt's *Mark Twain* plies the Rivers of America today.

Walt returned to California with pages of hand-written notes about a project he called Mickey Mouse Park. Walt often said of Disneyland, "It all started with a Mouse." But in a way, Disneyland also started with a train ride.

The Disneyland Railroad and Main Street Station

Walt's lifelong romance with trains is reflected in the prominent placement of the Railroad Station — a red brick Queen Anne-style structure with mansard roofs, railed roof walks, dormer windows, and a tall clock tower topped by an American flag. It's the first feature of Disneyland you see, even before you pass through the turnstile.

The Train Station harmonizes architecturally with the rest of Main Street USA. It's quaint, friendly, and

inviting. Climb the stairs and step inside Walt's train depot and you'll find:

- photos on the wall, illustrating the history of the
  Disneyland Railroad;

- a vintage coin-operated Nelson-Wiggen Orchestrion
  (a self-playing pipe organ operated by a music roll,
  producing additional sounds from a piano, xylo-
  phone, bass drums, and cymbals); and

- a replica of Walt's backyard live steam locomotive
  Lilly Belle (the original is at the Walt Disney Family
  Museum in San Francisco).

Step onto the platform, and you might see a yellow
Kalamazoo handcar on a siding. The handcar came from
Walt's own collection of railroad artifacts, and was prob-
ably a gift to Walt from railroad historian (and Warner
Bros. sound technologist) Gerald M. Best.

(In recent years, Walt's Kalamazoo handcar has been displayed at the Disney Family Museum in San Francisco and at other Disney- and railroad-related events. I saw it at the Fullerton Railroad Days in Fullerton, California, in May 2015, but I last saw it in the Park in March 2017, at New Orleans Square Station.)

Locomotive No. 5, Ward Kimball, *at Main Street Station.*

The Disneyland Railroad operates five steam locomotives on a three-foot narrow-gauge track. Four locomotives are named after Atchison, Topeka & Santa Fe Railroad presidents; one is named after Ward Kimball, who accompanied Walt to the Chicago Railroad Fair in 1948. The locomotives originally burned wood, coal, or heavy oil, but in 2007, they were converted to cleaner B98 biodiesel fuel (consisting of 2 percent diesel oil and 98 percent vegetable oil), made by recycling and filtering Disneyland's restaurant frying oils. (Some passengers say they can smell french fries when the train goes through a tunnel.)

The five Disneyland Railroad locomotives are:

No. 1, *C. K. Holliday*, named for Santa Fe Railroad founder Cyrus Kurtz Holliday. Built in the Disney Studio machine shop in 1954. The *Holliday* began service at Disneyland on opening day, July 17, 1955. It's based on Walt's backyard locomotive, the *Lilly Belle*, patterned after the Central Pacific No. 173 of the late 1800s.

Locomotive No. 2, E.P. Ripley
at New Orleans Square Station.

No. 2, *E. P. Ripley*, named for Edward Payson Ripley, an early president of the Atchison, Topeka and Santa Fe. Built in the studio machine shop in 1954, the *Ripley* also began service on opening day. It was patterned after the Baltimore and Ohio Railroad's No. 774 locomotive.

No. 3, *Fred Gurley*, named for Fred G. Gurley, president of the Atchison, Topeka and Santa Fe from 1944 to 1957. Built in 1894 by the Baldwin Locomotive Works of

Eddystone, Pennsylvania, the *Gurley* entered service at Disneyland on March 28, 1958. It's the oldest locomotive at any Disney theme park, and once hauled sugarcane in Louisiana.

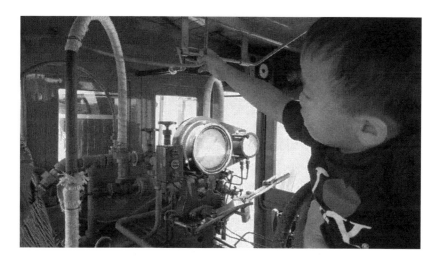

A young railroad enthusiast clangs the bell of Locomotive No. 4, Ernest S. Marsh.

No. 4, *Ernest S. Marsh*, named for Fred Gurley's successor, Ernest S. Marsh, a close friend of Walt's. Built by Baldwin Locomotive Works in 1925, the locomotive once hauled sand and passengers in New Jersey. Patterned after the Denver & Rio Grande's Montezuma locomotive, it began service at Disneyland on July 25, 1959.

No. 5, *Ward Kimball*, named for the Disney animator, was built by Baldwin Locomotive Works in 1902. It originally hauled sugarcane in Louisiana. Restored and refurbished, the *Kimball* began service at Disneyland on June 25, 2005, in time for the Park's fiftieth anniversary celebration. The locomotive's headlamp features a gold leaf silhouette of Jiminy Cricket, a character created for *Pinocchio* by Ward Kimball.

The first four locomotives are genuine artifacts of the Walt Disney era. Walt himself worked the throttle and blew the steam whistle of each of them. And he would certainly approve of naming the fifth after his friend and fellow railroad enthusiast, Ward Kimball.

Michael Broggie, son of Walt's railroad builder Roger Broggie, observed in *Walt Disney's Railroad Story*, "Walt Disney accumulated enough success and recognition for a dozen lifetimes. . . . His personal sense of pride and accomplishment was most evident when he climbed into the cab of a Disneyland locomotive. On board the *C. K. Holliday*, *E. P. Ripley*, *Fred Gurley*, or *Ernest S. Marsh*, he was the 'Chief Engineer' and sole owner of the Santa Fe and Disneyland Railroad, appropriately outfitted in Hercules bib overalls and jacket; a red bandanna; and — of course — an engineer's cap with its jauntily upturned bill."[1]

Oh, and here's a secret: *If* you arrive at Disneyland early enough, and go straight to the Train Station, and *if* Engine No. 1, the *C. K. Holliday*, or Engine No. 2, the *E. P. Ripley* is running that day, you and another guest may get to ride on the tender car, behind the locomotive. The tender seats put you right behind the cab with the engineer and fireman.

Why only those two trains? Because Engines 1 and 2 were built especially for Disneyland, and the tenders were designed by Walt to accommodate his guests. The other three trains, built decades earlier by Baldwin, weren't designed for hauling passengers around a theme park — so no tender seats.

Ask the Train Station cast member or train conductor. Remember, there may be a wait and tender seats aren't always available.

The Disneyland Railroad used to have a "combine" car (a coach with room for both passengers and baggage) called *Retlaw 1*. The car was named after Retlaw Enterprises, Walt's family-owned company that ran the trains, monorails, and *Mark Twain* steamboat in the early years of the Park (Retlaw is "Walter" spelled backwards). The *Retlaw 1* combine car was modeled after the Missouri Pacific combine where fourteen-year-old Walt took breaks while working as a candy butcher. Walt had warm memories of working on the railroad. The engineer and fireman often let him ride in the cab and blow the steam whistle. *Retlaw 1* was retired in 1974. It was sold in 2010 to the Carolwood Foundation and is now displayed next to Walt's Barn in Griffith Park.

Another unique Disneyland Railroad coach is the *Lilly Belle* presidential parlour car. The *Lilly Belle* was originally *Grand Canyon Observation Coach No. 106* when Disneyland opened in 1955. The original Disneyland train cars were fully enclosed, and the small windows made it difficult for Walt's guests to view the Grand Canyon diorama. So Walt replaced them with open cars that afforded a better view.

The Victorian interior of the Lilly Belle *(photo: HarshLight)*[2].

Walt ordered *No. 106* be refitted as a parlour car and renamed the *Lilly Belle* in honor of his wife Lillian. The interior is decorated in an elegant Victorian style: red velvet upholstery, mahogany paneling, beveled glass mirrors, stained glass, gold-fringed red-velvet drapes, gleaming brass accents, and marble tabletops.

The *Lilly Belle* is typically reserved for dignitaries, VIPs, and members of Disneyland's elite Club 33, though fortunate Disneyland guests are sometimes permitted aboard. Walt didn't live to ride aboard the *Lilly Belle* (which began service in 1975), but the parlour car was his idea, so it is very much a part of Walt's Disneyland.

All Disneyland Railroad rolling stock is housed and maintained at the Disneyland Roundhouse — a rectangular (not round) two-story building located in the northeast corner of the Disneyland property. (Traditionally, railroad roundhouses were round or semi-circular, and built around a turntable used to rotate the locomotives from one track to another.) The Disneyland Roundhouse is tucked between the "it's a small world" show building and the Santa Ana Freeway-Harbor Boulevard off-ramp.

The upper story of the Disneyland Roundhouse is the Monorail Shop, where the four Monorail trains are housed and maintained. The ground floor of the Roundhouse is where the five Disneyland steam locomotives and the fleet of passenger cars receive daily maintenance.

The Grand Canyon and Primeval World

One of the most popular attractions along the Disneyland Railroad is the Grand Canyon and Primeval World diorama, located between the Tomorrowland and Main Street stations. The diorama was created in 1958 by Delmer J. Yoakum, a Hollywood designer and scenery painter who worked on such films as *The Shoes of the Fisherman*, *The King and I*, *Niagara*, and Hitchcock's *North by Northwest* (remember the Mount Rushmore scene?). Yoakum also worked on such Disneyland attractions as Pirates of the Caribbean, the Haunted Mansion, and "it's a small world."

Yoakum painted the Grand Canyon and Primeval World diorama on a seamless canvas that is three stories high and longer than a football field. He used 300 gallons of paint in fourteen colors to create the realistic image, which depicts the view from the Grand Canyon's south rim. The scene is populated with taxidermied deer, bighorn sheep, a mountain lion, a golden eagle, skunk, porcupine, and wild turkeys.

The third movement of Ferde Grofé's "Grand Canyon Suite" provides the soundtrack. Chief Nevangnewa, a ninety-six-year-old Hopi Native American, blessed the trains and the diorama on the day the exhibit opened.

The diorama was expanded with the addition of the Primeval World section in 1966, inspired by the "Rite of Spring" segment of the 1940 animated feature *Fantasia*. The Primeval World displays a number of Audio-Animatronic dinosaurs, recreations of creatures that existed in different prehistoric eras: a sail-backed Edaphosaurus from the late Carboniferous period (300 million years ago), a Meganeura (giant dragonfly) also from the Carboniferous, a Brontosaurus from the Kimmeridgian age (about 155 million years ago), a cliff-perched Pteranodon from the late Cretaceous period (68 million years ago), a three horned mama Triceratops standing guard over her hatchlings (also from the late Cretaceous), a herd of ostrich-like late Cretaceous Struthiomimus by a watering hole, and near the end of the diorama, battling to the death next to a glowing lava pit, a Tyrannosaurus Rex (late Cretaceous) and a Stegosaurus (late Jurassic).

The Tyrannosaur in the Primeval World (like the one in *Fantasia*) has three-fingered (or three-clawed) hands. Actual prehistoric Tyrannosaurs only had two claws on each hand. Walt knew that his Tyrannosaurs, in both the film and the Disneyland diorama, were anatomically incorrect, but he had the artists add one claw to each hand because he thought it made the creatures seem fiercer.

The Primeval World dinosaurs were originally part of Walt Disney's Ford Magic Skyway attraction, one of four attractions Disney built for the 1964 New York World's Fair. The other World's Fair attractions — Great Moments with Mr. Lincoln, the Carousel of Progress, and "it's a small world" — also came to Disneyland after the World's Fair closed in 1965.

Dreams Made of Concrete, Stone, and Steel

Walt spared no expense in perfecting a motion picture or his theme park. Yet he wanted to lavish his spending on the "show." It rankled him that so much of his construction budget went to concrete foundations and infrastructure sunk into the ground. A few months before opening day, with tears in his eyes, Walt complained to Harper Goff, "I've spent half the budget already, and there isn't one thing you'd call terrific out there right now."

In early 1955, Walt toured the Disneyland property with construction supervisor Joe Fowler. Standing at the site of the Main Street train station while workers poured the concrete foundation over steel rebar, Walt turned to Fowler and complained, "Joe, by the time you've buried all my money in the ground, I won't have enough left to put on a show!"

Walt wanted to amaze and astound his guests with this fully immersive show called Disneyland. Don Rake, a transportation engineer who assisted Imagineer Roger Broggie in designing the Disneyland Railroad, recorded his impressions from his first tour of the Disneyland construction site with Broggie.

"As we talked and walked," Rake said, "Roger pointed to the Main Street storefronts. He explained that Walt insisted on complete second story construction, no false fronts and façades, no sham in any way. He told me that all construction was a 'complete build out' with quality materials. He explained that the Castle could have been built with wire mesh frame and gunite. It would have looked natural, but Walt insisted that it be made with solid limestone blocks and mortar. This tour was a real education into the goals and character of Walt Disney."

When Walt built dreams out of concrete and stone, he spared no expense and he built to last. As Don Rake concluded, "Walt was a perfectionist."[3]

All the nostalgic vehicles that carry guests along Main Street were designed and built by Imagineer Bob Gurr in the machine shop at the Disney Studio in Burbank.

On opening day in 1955, there were three horse-drawn vehicles on Main Street. Two have since been retired, the horse-drawn Fire Wagon (retired in 1960, now on display in the Fire House), and the wooden-wheeled Surrey (retired in 1971).

Today, four vehicles take guests up and down Main Street:

The Horse-Drawn Street Car — a turn-of-the-century trolley, weighing two tons and pulled by a single strong horse (usually a Percheron or a Belgian; you can find the horse's name imprinted on the bridle). Horses are worked gently, just four hours a day, four days a week. The trolley is the only Main Street vehicle that was operating on opening day, July 17, 1955, and it has remained unchanged ever since (except for the removal of the 10 cent fare box; like all Disneyland attractions, it's now free with admission). The horse-drawn trolley can transport up to thirty passengers at speeds of nearly five miles an hour. It operates in the morning and early afternoon, but is removed from Main Street before the first parade of the day.

The Horseless Carriage — the 1903 vintage "jitney" carries up to six passengers. The red Horseless Carriage first appeared on Main Street on May 12, 1956; its yellow companion first appeared on December 6, 1956. The Horseless Carriages are not based on any single historic vehicle, but are composites of several different gasoline-powered cars of that period.

The Omnibus[4] — an open-air two-story bus modeled after New York's Fifth Avenue double-deckers of the 1920s. Though the Omnibus is a faithful reproduction of turn-of-the-century busses, its drop-frame chassis, power steering, and power brakes are modern adaptations. The seating was also modified for a more comfortable ride and a better view. The electric klaxon horn is an authentic antique. Introduced in August 1956, the Omnibus carries up to forty-five passengers in comfort and style.

The Fire Engine — a replica of an early 20th century fire engine (based on a 1916 American LaFrance). The Fire Engine was Walt's favorite vehicle, and he often drove it around Disneyland before the Park opened for the day. Originally gasoline-powered, the Fire Engine now runs on cleaner-burning natural gas. Passenger seats occupy the space where hoses and fire-fighting equipment are traditionally stowed. Originally fitted with a siren, the vehicle's only noisemakers are now an antique bell and horn.

The Fire Engine is the only Main Street vehicle that wasn't Walt's original idea. It was suggested by vehicle designer Bob Gurr, who constructed it at the Burbank studio, then personally drove it down the Santa Ana Freeway to Disneyland. The Fire Engine began service on Main Street on August 15, 1958.

Walt Disney was fascinated by every form of transportation you can imagine, from pirate ships and steam trains to rocket ships and futuristic Monorails. Walt's nostalgic memories of the past seem to center on various forms of transportation — and so did his optimistic dreams of the future.

In 1949, Walt Disney released an animated adaptation of Kenneth Grahame's *The Wind in the Willows* (as part of a package film called *The Adventures of Ichabod and Mr. Toad*). It tells of the calamities that befall the compulsive J. Thaddeus Toad, master of Toad Hall. Mr. Toad is driven by assorted manias, and he's especially obsessed with this newfangled invention known as a motorcar. His car bears a striking resemblance to the 1903 Horseless Carriage on Main Street USA. In both the movie and the Fantasyland dark ride, Mr. Toad lives out Walt's mania for machines of transportation.

When visiting Disneyland with your family, and especially with children or grandchildren, you'll want to enrich their experience of Walt's Disneyland by sharing with them the history of Walt's steam trains, his Main Street vehicles, and the other transportation systems around the Park. Ask questions of drivers, conductors, and other cast members. Better yet, encourage the children to ask questions. Most cast members are eager to talk about the history of Disneyland's Main Street, and the historic era it represents.

CHAPTER FIVE

Walt's Adventureland

*"To create a land that would make this dream reality,
we pictured ourselves far from civilization, in the remote
jungles of Asia and Africa."*
—*Walt Disney*

In mid-1941, Walt received a visitor from the United States government — Nelson Rockefeller, Coordinator for Inter-American Affairs in the FDR White House. Rockefeller met with Walt in his Burbank office and told him the government was concerned about unrest and pro-Axis sentiment in Latin America. Though America had not yet entered World War II (the attack on Pearl Harbor was just months away), President Roosevelt wanted to keep enemy influence out of the western hemisphere.

"Your movies are popular in Latin America," Rockefeller said. "You can help offset the Nazi influence if you'll go down there and show the people what America is all about." Walt agreed, and — along with his wife and fifteen animators and other associates — he departed from Los Angeles airport on August 11, 1941. Walt explained his reasons for going to Latin America this way: "While half of this world is being forced to shout 'Heil Hitler,' our answer is to say, 'Saludos Amigos.' "[1]

Walt draws Goofy for children in Argentina
(photo: Archivo General de la Nación Argentina).

Walt and his entourage flew to Belém, Brazil, gateway to the lower Amazon region, where they spent several days. Their tour then took them to Rio, Buenos Aires, and Santiago, plus stops in Peru, Ecuador, and Colombia. They visited zoos and farms, attended concerts and art galleries, explored beaches and rain forests, learned to samba and rumba, and crossed Lake Titicaca in balsawood boats.

Walt set up his base of operations at the Alvear Palace Hotel, a historic luxury hotel in Buenos Aires. He and his artists furnished a well-equipped art studio on the roof. The sketches and paintings they produced during that tour would become the basis of two Latin American-themed animated films, *Saludos Amigos* (1942) and *The Three Caballeros* (1944).

The Latin American goodwill tour also inspired one of the four original lands of Disneyland — Adventureland. It's a land devoted to the natural wonders and exotic wildlife of South America, Africa, Asia, and the South Pacific. A thirty-mile steamer cruise up a jungle river in Colombia inspired a popular Adventureland attraction, The Jungle Cruise. The river boats in The Jungle Cruise are scaled-down versions of the river steamer Walt boarded for his Colombian jungle cruise.

Adventureland is themed to evoke the jungles and rain forests of the equatorial world. In the planning stages, Walt named this land True-Life Adventureland, after his True-Life Adventures, a series of short nature films and feature-length documentaries produced from 1948 to 1960. He wanted this land to be a living documentary, populated with live animals, so that people could experience a "true-life" rainforest adventure. When it became clear that it would not be feasible to keep live animals in this land, he dropped "True-Life" from the name and called it Adventureland.

Walt wanted each land in Disneyland to have a tall structure to attract crowds. As we saw in Chapter 3, he called these eye-catching structures "wienies." Adventureland is the only original land in the Park without a "wienie" — yet Walt had always planned to build one. (The Treehouse is not a true "wienie." Though it is certainly tall, the Treehouse blends into the tree-line of Adventureland rather than towering over it.)

Walt originally envisioned a glass-enclosed attraction called the Arboretum to tower over Adventureland — but he never built it. The first Disneyland souvenir guidebook, published in 1955, showed the proposed site of the Arboretum, to the right of the entrance to the Jungle Cruise boathouse. The Arboretum would have been designed with tall golden spires like those of a temple in Thailand or Cambodia. The towering Arboretum would have housed exotic plants and birds, and rivaled Sleeping Beauty Castle in height.

The Arboretum project was canceled before the Park opened, a casualty of the soaring cost of building the Park. The Arboretum quietly disappeared from the 1956 Disneyland guidebook and was never mentioned again.

Adventureland attractions conceived and built under Walt's personal direction are The Jungle Cruise (opened July 17, 1955), the Swiss Family Treehouse (opened November 18, 1962; rethemed as Tarzan's Treehouse in 1999), and the Enchanted Tiki Room (opened June 23, 1963). In 1995, the Indiana Jones Adventure opened, marking the first major addition to Adventureland since Walt's death.

The Big Game Safari Shooting Gallery opened in 1962, allowing guests to shoot BB pellets at "big game" targets. Unfortunately, the BBs tended to ricochet off the targets and sting passing guests. Another problem: the targets had to be hand-painted nightly due to BB damage. The Shooting Gallery closed in 1982 and the space was turned into a gift shop. (A similar shooting gallery in Frontierland is still in operation today, using safer, more cost-effective laser-guns instead of BB-guns.)

A grassy area next to The Jungle Cruise was once known as Magnolia Park. Concerts were performed at the Magnolia Park bandstand from July 1956 until the little park closed in 1962 for the Elephant Bathing Pool expansion of The Jungle Cruise.

Now for a tour of Walt's Adventureland . . .

The Jungle Cruise

The Jungle Cruise was Walt's brainchild and one of his favorite attractions — a nostalgic tribute to his 1941 Colombian cruise. He was committed to having The Jungle Cruise ready on opening day. Walt had originally planned to populate the attraction with live animals, but animal experts told him that jungle creatures were difficult to control, expensive to maintain, and potentially dangerous. They also liked to sleep during the day. So Walt enlisted his studio special effects team to produce lifelike mechanical hippos, lions, elephants, birds, and other creatures — a metal-and-latex menagerie that would perform on schedule.

Most of the credit for the realistic feel of The Jungle Cruise goes to Disneyland's chief botanist and landscaper Bill Evans. He devised creative approaches to building his jungle, using a combination of live exotic plants, artificial plants, and even uprooted orange trees planted upside down. The roots of trees that had been bulldozed when the original orchard was cleared looked a lot like jungle vines, branches, and creepers. Evans also used both living and artificial plants to hide speakers, wires, pipes, and structures.

While Walt was building Disneyland, the state of California was busily expanding its freeway system. Evans and his crew secured many mature palm trees that had been tagged for destruction by state surveyors.

Though Walt's inspiration was his South American river cruise, the attraction's chief designer, Harper Goff, was inspired by the 1951 motion picture *The African Queen*, based on the novel by C. S. Forester and starring Humphrey Bogart and Katherine Hepburn. The cruise simulates four different rivers of the world — the Amazon River of South America, the Congo and Nile rivers of Africa, and the Mekong River of Southeast Asia.

Dick Nunis took a summer job as one of Disneyland's first attraction operators in 1955. That summer job became a career. He retired in 1999 as director of park operations. One of his first jobs at Disneyland was foreman of The Jungle Cruise. Soon after the Park opened, Walt arrived at the dock for a surprise inspection and boarded a cruise boat with other Disneyland guests.

As the boat left the dock, Nunis watched anxiously. When the boat returned a few minutes later, Walt stepped off — and he was not happy. "Dick," he said, "how long is that Cruise supposed to take?"

"Seven minutes," Nunis replied.

"I timed it at just over four minutes," Walt said. "We shot through there so fast, I couldn't tell the elephants from the hippos!"

So Nunis put his team of boat operators through a refresher course. The cruise operators practiced until they could make the trip in exactly seven minutes every time without fail.

A few days later, Walt returned for another surprise inspection. Nunis called his best cruise operators to the front, hoping Walt would be satisfied with a single test ride. No such luck. Walt rode and timed every boat and every operator — and each cruise lasted precisely seven minutes. That's a testament to how much Walt cared about the attraction and the guest experience.

When Pat Williams and I researched *How to Be Like Walt*, former Disneyland cast member John Catone told us, "I often saw Walt around the Park early in the morning. He'd be dressed in blue jeans and a straw hat, with a red handkerchief around his neck. He'd tour the Park, talk to the ride operators, and check on everything. One day, I took Walt on The Jungle Cruise and I noticed that I could see the hippo's mechanical parts in the clear water. I said, 'Look, Walt, you can see the mechanism.' He frowned and took note of it. A few days later, the water was dark and murky, and the hippo looked as real as could be. Walt had taken care of the problem."

You're probably familiar with the pun-laden spiel the boat operators deliver: "We're approaching the beautiful Schweitzer Falls, named after the famous explorer, Dr. Albert Falls. . . . And here we see the backside of Schweitzer Falls, named for the backside of the famous explorer, Dr. Albert Falls. . . . We're now entering the Nile River, the longest river in all of Anaheim."

The original spiel, when the Park opened, was more realistic and documentary-style, with just a few gentle touches of humor. Walt originally envisioned The Jungle Cruise as a full-immersion educational adventure — a realistic journey through the rivers of the equatorial South America, Africa, and Asia. The spiel, and the cruise itself, have evolved over time.

Disney historian Jim Hill recounts the story of when Walt was making one of his incognito visits to Disneyland in the late 1950s. While walking through Adventureland, Walt overheard a mother tell her child, "We don't need to go on The Jungle Cruise this time — we saw it the last time we were here." That comment stuck in Walt's craw. He immediately assigned his Imagineers to the task of improving the attraction.

This is an example of a concept Walt called "plussing." It's the near-fanatical commitment to continuously improving Disneyland. As long as Disney Imagineers keep plussing the Disneyland experience, his guests will always have a reason to return and re-experience iconic attractions like The Jungle Cruise.[2]

Originally a D-ticket attraction, The Jungle Cruise was upgraded when E-tickets were introduced in June 1959. The coupon books were phased out by mid-1982.

(A tip: When you complete your cruise, ask a cast member for a free Jungle Cruise map. I'm told the cast member may ask you for a joke in trade for the map, so here's one for you: Why did Captain Hook cross the road? To get to the second-hand store.)

The Little Man of Disneyland

In 1955, Little Golden Books published *Little Man of Disneyland* by Annie North Bedford (the pen name for Golden Books editor Jane Werner). The book is illustrated by animator Dick Kelsey, a veteran of such films as *Pinocchio*, *Fantasia*, and *Alice in Wonderland*.

The story introduces Patrick Begorra, a leprechaun living in the trunk of an orange tree in Anaheim. One day, the peace and quiet of the orange grove is disturbed by a construction crew consisting of Mickey Mouse, Donald Duck, Pluto, and Goofy. They are uprooting orange trees and clearing the land for a project called Disneyland. Patrick's home is in the path of the demolition.

The little man is horrified at the prospect of losing his home and his orange grove. So Mickey and Co. take the leprechaun to Burbank for a tour of the Disney Studio. They show him the plans for Disneyland, and he sees "rows of pretty little shops, winding rivers, an overhead railroad train — so many wonderful things."

Patrick says, "This is what you are planning to build when you root up my orange trees? . . . Then go ahead, lads. . . . The place is yours. There's just one little thing I ask. May I build me a wee snug little house and live on there quietly after you have finished this Disneyland?"

So Patrick Begorra lives in Disneyland to this day, and his hidden tree trunk home is somewhere in Adventureland. *Little Man of Disneyland* is still in print, so you can read it to your children, then take them to Adventureland to find Patrick's home. Hint: look near the entrance to the Indiana Jones Adventure — and have your camcorder ready.

Oh, and between you and me, Patrick's home was added in August 2015. Because of its connection to the classic 1955 Golden Book, I'm including Patrick's home as an authentic piece of Walt's Disneyland.

The Treehouse

In 1960, Disney released the motion picture *Swiss Family Robinson*, based on the 1812 novel by Johann David Wyss. Starring John Mills, Dorothy McGuire, James MacArthur, Janet Munro, Tommy Kirk, and Kevin Corcoran, the film depicts members of a shipwrecked family rebuilding their lives on a tropical island. The Swiss Family Treehouse opened two years later in Adventureland. The walk-through attraction was co-designed by Imagineer Bill Martin and artist Wolfgang Reitherman, who designed the treehouse for the movie.

The tree and Treehouse are constructed of reinforced steel and concrete. The skeleton of the structure stands sixty feet tall and the foliage reaches seventy feet in height. The attraction weighs more than 150 tons. Guests walk up wooden stairs and cross rope bridges to view various rooms, as depicted in the film. The rooms are decorated with items salvaged from the shipwreck or found along the beach. The tree is adorned with more than 150,000 vinyl leaves and more than 50,000 flowers. The tree is the only known specimen of its species, which Disneyland botanists call *Disneyodendron semperflorens grandis*.

In its original Swiss Family version, an ingenious and fully functioning plumbing system provided running water to the Treehouse by means of a waterwheel, a series of cups, and bamboo pipes. The water system lifted 200 gallons of water up into the Treehouse every hour. Gravity distributed the water through bamboo gutters to every room in the Treehouse. It was an inspired bit of castaway engineering.

Walt conceived the attraction as a walk-through — or, more precisely, a climb-through. There are sixty-eight steps going up, sixty-nine going down. When Walt pitched his idea to the Imagineers at WED Enterprises, they predicted failure. No one, they said, would want to climb all the way to the top of the Treehouse, then wend their way back down again. Walt's reply: Everybody loves a treehouse. And, of course, he was right.

Some of my happiest memories were formed when my brothers and I built a treehouse in a backyard sycamore tree. There's just something about climbing up into the branches of a tree that brings joy to a child's heart. Walt understood — and he pressed ahead with his Treehouse in Adventureland.

While the Treehouse may not be as popular as, say, The Jungle Cruise, it has welcomed countless visitors, young and old, who love the notion of living high in a tree, surrounded by the comforts of home. The Swiss Family Treehouse held an iconic place in Adventureland, and the music from the Swiss Family pump organ — a lively tune called "Swisskapolka" — used to fill the air.

John Mills, who starred as Father Robinson in the film, was on hand (with daughter Hayley Mills) for the 1962 opening of the attraction. The walk-through cost a C-ticket at the time, was demoted to a B-ticket attraction in 1966, and is now free with admission to the Park.

Beginning in February 1999, Disneyland gave the Treehouse a makeover, retheming it as Tarzan's Treehouse. The Treehouse reopened on June 23, 1999, roughly coinciding with the release of Disney's animated *Tarzan* feature. But while the Swiss Family Treehouse was a genuine homage to a Disney motion picture, Tarzan's Treehouse felt more like a promotional display. Imagineers remembered the original Swiss Family version by playing a tinny-sounding Victrola recording of "Swisskapolka." But too much of the original Treehouse atmosphere disappeared during the makeover.

Gone was the fascinating waterwheel-and-gravity plumbing system of the original Treehouse. Gone, too, was the *sense of place* that the original Treehouse gave you — the illusion of being physically *in the movie*. It was as if those who created the Tarzan makeover didn't grasp the mind of Walt Disney.

Every attraction Walt himself created for the Park was designed to put *you*, Walt's guest, in the starring role. You are not merely a spectator — Disneyland is a choose-your-own-adventure experience and *you* are the star. Whether you're riding a trolley down Main Street USA circa 1910, or flying off to Never Land with Peter Pan, or soaring into space aboard the Moonliner, you are fully immersed in the time and place of that adventure.

That was Walt's idea behind the Swiss Family Treehouse. Climbing those steps, *you* became part of that castaway family, living in that tree, exploring its rooms, reliving the Swiss Family Robinson's adventures. You were immersed in the experience. The Tarzan-themed makeover did away with that illusion — an illusion that is central to Walt's idea of Disneyland.

There's nothing wrong with the Tarzan motif per se. The problem is that it alters the role of Walt's guests. Instead of being the stars of our own adventure, we're demoted to the role of spectators in a Tarzan museum. The rooms of the treehouse are decorated with characters and creatures from the animated film — motionless figures of Tarzan, Jane, and assorted jungle animals. Personal opinion: I don't think Walt would approve.[3]

Still, the Treehouse is worth experiencing. When you look out through the foliage at Frontierland, the Rivers of America, and New Orleans Square, you can still see it all through the eyes of Walt Disney.

The Enchanted Tiki Room

Here's a fun fact: The Enchanted Tiki Room is the only attraction in Disneyland with its own restrooms. This is because Walt originally envisioned the Tiki Room as a restaurant with a floor show of singing, talking birds and flowers. At its inception, the Tiki Room was privately owned by Walt, and there was a 75 cent cover charge due to the separate ownership. The Park's E-ticket attractions, such as the Matterhorn Bobsleds, were only 50 cents. So Walt's Tiki Room was a premium attraction.

The Tiki Room was inspired by a discovery Walt made in an antique shop in New Orleans: a mechanical bird in a gilded cage. The bird flapped its wings, fluttered its tail, moved its head, and opened its beak. Walt knew that if an antique contraption could do all that, his Imagineers could improve it a hundredfold.

Walt bought the mechanical bird and took it home to California. The day he showed that bird to his Imagineers was the day Audio-Animatronics was born.

To Walt, Audio-Animatronics took two-dimensional animation into the third dimension. He said, "We are using the new type of valves and controls developed for rockets. That way we can create extremely subtle motions. . . . Everything is preprogramed on tape: the bird's movements, lighting effects, and sound. We turn on the tape and the birds do their stuff. At the end, the tape automatically rewinds itself and starts all over again."

The technology behind The Enchanted Tiki Room, Walt said, is "just animation with sound, run by electronics. It's an extension of animated drawings. We take an inanimate object and make it move."[4]

(Photo: HarshLight)[5]

The show features four macaws from four different countries: José from Mexico (voiced by longtime Disneyland performer Wally Boag), Michael from Ireland (Fulton Burley). Pierre from France (Ernie Newton), and Fritz from Germany (Thurl Ravenscroft). In addition to the four stars of the show, there are more than 225 birds, flowers, and tiki idols. They perform such songs as "In the Tiki Room" (by the Sherman Brothers), "Let's All Sing Like the Birdies Sing," and "The Hawaiian War Chant." The Soprano Orchid in the "War Chant" is voiced by Norma Zimmer, famed as *The Lawrence Welk Show*'s "Champagne Lady."

The four macaws appear to breathe as they talk and sing. This is because their chest plumage is covered with a woven cashmere material that naturally expands and contracts. The Imagineers had been searching for a way to achieve this realistic touch when Walt accidentally gave them the solution. During a meeting, Imagineer Harriet Burns noticed that Walt's blue cashmere sweater expanded and contracted at the elbows in exactly the manner she was looking for. Problem solved.

The script and music of today's Tiki Room show are largely unchanged since the attraction opened June 23, 1963. The only upgrade is the addition of digitally remastered sound and improved Audio-Animatronics, which were added in time for Disneyland's fiftieth anniversary celebration in 2005. The Enchanted Tiki Room is a near-pristine holdover from Walt's day.

Before being seated for the show, guests wait in the lanai where Hawaiian music plays. The Dole Snack Bar dispenses pineapple drinks and snacks (the most popular, especially on a hot day, is the frosty Dole Whip).

Adventureland attractions that have disappeared since Walt's death include the Tahitian Terrace (opened 1962, closed 1993; a Polynesian-themed dinner show that was replaced by Aladdin's Oasis) and the Big Game Safari Shooting Gallery (opened 1962, closed 1982).

Apart from the addition of the Indiana Jones Adventure in 1995 and the re-theming of the Treehouse in 1999, Adventureland remains much as Walt left it. Be enchanted by the Tiki Room and explore the rivers of The Jungle Cruise, and you'll experience Adventureland as Walt himself created it — and enjoyed it.

Choose your own adventure in Walt's Adventureland.

CHAPTER SIX

Walt's Frontierland

"Frontierland. It is here that we experience the story of our country's past. The color, romance, and drama of Frontier America as it developed from wilderness trails to roads, riverboats, and civilization. A tribute to the faith, courage, and ingenuity of our hardy pioneers who blazed the trails and made this progress possible."
—*Walt Disney*

Walt found his success at a time when America was losing its way — the Great Depression. Many who had invested in Wall Street lost everything. But Walt didn't invest in the stock market. He invested in *himself* and his own dreams. He turned the Disney Studio into a thriving American success story at a time when Wall Street was in panic and the banks were failing left and right.

But Walt's success came at a price. While his most famous creation, Mickey Mouse, was enjoying global popularity, Walt himself was struggling with stress and depression. In 1931, Walt suffered a breakdown, and he checked into Good Samaritan Hospital in Los Angeles.

The doctors told him he needed to take some time away from the pressures of his studio.

So Walt took Lillian off on a "gypsy jaunt," an unplanned excursion to take his mind off of studio business for a few weeks. They boarded a train in Los Angeles, bound for St. Louis. There, they planned to take a riverboat down the Mississippi to New Orleans.

Arriving in St. Louis, they found that the Mississippi River boats were no longer running. The Great Depression had put them out of business. It was a blow to Walt's spirit. Since his boyhood, when reading the stories of Mark Twain, he had dreamed of riding the Mississippi on a stern paddlewheel riverboat.

It would be more than two decades before he would realize that dream — and he'd have to build the riverboat himself. Today, the riverboat Walt built, the *Mark Twain*, is the signature attraction of Frontierland.

The spirit of Walt Disney is the spirit of the American frontier. He was continually moving out, expanding his horizons, daring the impossible, never doubting himself or his vision, even while the rest of the world was in panic. Frontierland is a metaphor of America's mythic and heroic past — and a metaphor of Walt's own belief in the power of rugged American individualism.

Making Memories on the Riverboat

The *Mark Twain* is a five-eighths scale riverboat that takes passengers on a twelve-minute scenic journey along the Rivers of America. There are few attractions in Disneyland that better reflect the soul of Walt himself than the *Mark Twain*. As far back as the early 1930s, when Walt first imagined a theme park across from his

Burbank studio, his earliest sketches included a Mississippi riverboat ride.

When Walt began building Disneyland, it had been fifty years since a paddle wheeler had been built anywhere in the United States. Riverboat-building was a lost art. Walt's designers researched the historical literature on paddle wheelers, and drew up plans for the kind of riverboat that plied the Mississippi during Mark Twain's day.

As Disneyland's costs mounted, Roy told Walt that construction of the *Mark Twain* should wait until after the Park opened. Walt wouldn't hear of it. He was so determined to have his riverboat that he financed it out of his own pocket.

The 105-foot hull of the *Mark Twain* was constructed at Todd Shipyards in San Pedro, California, and the superstructure and decks were built at the Disney Studio in Burbank. Constructing the boat in pieces at two locations might seem to be an invitation to Murphy's Law. But when all the parts were assembled in Frontierland, they fit together perfectly.

Walt's construction supervisor, retired admiral Joe
Fowler, insisted on building a drydock for the riverboat
along the Rivers of America. Dismayed at the expense of
a drydock, Walt labeled it "Joe's Ditch" and "Fowler's
Harbor." The drydock is still called Fowler's Harbor today, and the three-masted sailing ship *Columbia* (built
in 1958) anchors there. The drydock facilities are disguised by a façade called Fowler's Inn, a ramshackle-
looking establishment with a leaning front porch. It is
located across the walkway from the Haunted Mansion.

One of Disneyland's lesser-known eateries saved
Fowler's Inn from the wrecking ball in the late 1980s.
When Disneyland execs wanted to demolish the Fowler's
Inn façade to accommodate an expanded restaurant in
Critter Country, one Disneyland planner suggested an
alternative: Add a walk-up restaurant to the Fowler's
Inn area. Today, tucked away beside Fowler's Harbor is
Harbour Galley, a walk-up chowder-and-sandwich res-
taurant. There's not much seating, but the lines are usu-
ally short. Harbour Galley opened in 1989, so it's not part
of "Walt's Disneyland," yet the tiny eatery deserves
credit for saving Fowler's Harbor — an important part of
Walt's Disneyland — from demolition.

(Few people know about the "Harbour Galley Secret
Path." Walk around the waterfront side of the Harbour
Galley building. The path will take you past the Fowler's
Harbor façade, and up to a walkway where you'll have
an excellent view of Splash Mountain's steep drop into
the briar patch and the logs floating down the flume.)

The *Mark Twain* departs every twenty-five minutes
from a sheltered loading dock. Historic flags of the
United States fly over the entrance. After boarding the
Mark Twain, passengers can move freely on its three

decks. The lower deck has chairs in the bow, and the top deck provides an excellent view of the waterfront sights.

The pilot operates the Mark Twain from the wheelhouse, which is furnished with a ship's wheel, whistle, bell controls, and the captain's bed. The wheelhouse of the *Mark Twain* was one of Walt's favorite places in Disneyland.

The riverboat is controlled by an I-beam guide rail hidden by the murky water, so the pilot doesn't have to steer. But the pilot does have to watch for river traffic, such as Davy Crockett's Explorer Canoes and the rafts taking guests to Tom Sawyer Island. The pilot also communicates commands to the boiler engineer, who controls the throttle and reverse gear.

A memory-making tip for parents: On arriving at the dock, inform a cast member that you'd like to have your kids ride in the wheelhouse with the pilot. At the pilot's discretion, and if no other guests have reserved that privilege ahead of you, your kids can ride in the wheelhouse and "steer" the boat. They'll also sign the guestbook and receive a personalized souvenir Pilot's License.

Narration along the journey is delivered by Thurl Ravenscroft (who is heard all around Disneyland, and who was also the voice of Kellogg's Tony the Tiger). Actor Stephen Stanton is the voice of the captain, and actor Peter Renaday provides the voice of Mark Twain. The narration points out such landmarks as the Haunted Mansion, Splash Mountain, the settler's cabin (which burned continually throughout my boyhood, but no longer burns today), the Indian village, Big Thunder Mountain, and more.[1]

The *Mark Twain*'s maiden voyage took place on July 13, 1955, four days before Disneyland's opening day. Three hundred invited guests attended a private party for Walt and Lillian's thirtieth wedding anniversary. The party began with a show at the Golden Horseshoe Saloon and concluded with an evening riverboat cruise.

Joe Fowler wanted to make sure the *Mark Twain* was ready to launch. When he arrived at the dock, he found Lillian alone on the deck, broom in hand, sweeping sawdust and debris. Fowler picked up another broom and helped Mrs. Disney sweep the deck.

During the live television broadcast of Disneyland's opening day, actress Irene Dunne (star of the movie *Showboat*) stood on the foredeck of the *Mark Twain*. Alongside her was Walt's co-host Art Linkletter. Holding a ribbon-festooned bottle, she said, "This bottle contains waters from all the leading rivers in America. So with these precious waters, I christen this boat the *Mark Twain!*" And she smashed the bottle against the capstan.

Admiral Fowler was in the wheelhouse as captain during the riverboat's first official voyage. No one had thought to determine a maximum capacity for the boat, so throughout that cruise, the overloaded boat would list to port or starboard as the crowd rushed from side to side to view the passing scenery.

On one trip during the first week of operation, ride operators allowed more than five hundred guests to board, causing the boat to ride dangerously low in the water. During the trip, the boat came loose from its I-beam track and drifted up against the muddy banks. The *Mark Twain* had to be evacuated, and a maximum capacity of three hundred passengers has been enforced ever since.

In the early years of the *Mark Twain*'s operation, passengers could purchase a non-alcoholic mint julep to sip, and the Disneyland band would entertain passengers with Dixieland jazz on the lower deck. In recent years, the iron grillwork between the smokestacks has been reshaped to incorporate a "hidden Mickey."

Walt's Shrinking Wilderness

From Central Plaza, you enter Frontierland through a stockade gate made of ponderosa pine logs. Passing the storefronts of the Frontier Trading Post, Silver Spur

Supplies, the Crockett and Russel Hat Co. (with a window honoring actor Fess Parker), and the Pioneer Mercantile, you see the Rivers of America before you, with the twin smokestacks of the *Mark Twain*.

Frontierland presents an idealized image of the American Old West — a region that once stretched from the western banks of the Mississippi, across the painted canyons and deserts of the American Southwest, all the way to the gold rush towns of California. As Walt originally conceived it, Frontierland was not dense with attractions, but contained open expanses of wilderness that guests could explore by stagecoach, pack mules, steam train, and hiking trails.

The stagecoaches and pack mules have vanished. So have the four-times-daily gunfights in the street in front of the Golden Horseshoe Saloon, in which the Sheriff always got the drop on Black Bart. The gunfights began on opening day and ended in 1963.

Walt's wilderness began shrinking within his lifetime, a sacrifice to his constant quest to add new attractions. In 1960, the Mine Train Through Nature's Wonderland (an expansion of the 1956 attraction Rainbow Caverns Mine Train) sent Walt's stagecoaches and Conestoga wagons to the boneyard, and put the pack mules out to pasture. The Mine Train was replaced in 1979 by the Big Thunder Mountain Railroad thrill ride.

Though I'm a Big Thunder Mountain fan, I do miss the Mine Train — a leisurely train ride through the Old West. A scaled-down steam locomotive pulled mine cars through a tunnel and out onto the Rainbow Desert, which featured Disney versions of natural wonders such as a giant saguaro cactus forest, the Devil's Paint Pots,

Ol' Unfaithful geyser, and balancing rocks that teetered when the train whistle blew.

The grand finale, Rainbow Caverns, was a two-minute dark ride. The caverns featured stalactites and stalagmites, luminous geysers, a multicolored waterfall, a bubbling fountain called Witch's Cauldron, and more. The UV black light effects made the colors in the caverns all the more dramatic.

When the Big Thunder Mountain Railroad opened in 1979, portions of the old Mine Train route and scenery (such as the mining town buildings) were retained in the new attraction. Unfortunately, the eye-dazzling colors of Rainbow Caverns, created by artist Claude Coats, are gone forever.

In 1972, a new themed land, Bear Country, replaced Walt's original Indian Village section of Frontierland. Bear Country was renamed Critter Country in 1988.

Though much of Walt's Frontierland has vanished, some vintage Frontierland attractions remain, as great as ever. The Golden Horseshoe Saloon, for example, was open for business on Disneyland's opening day in 1955, and still entertains audiences today. Overlooking the waterfront, the Golden Horseshoe Saloon has been home to several popular stage productions.

The original stage show, "Slue Foot Sue's Golden Horseshoe Revue," was written and performed by Donald Novis and Wally Boag. After Novis became ill in 1962, Fulton Burley took over the role. The show ran for more than 39,000 performances from July 17, 1955 until October 12, 1986, and was listed by the *Guinness Book of Records* as the longest-running musical of all time.

The Golden Horseshoe Saloon was designed by Harper Goff, a multi-talented Renaissance man — artist, scene designer, musician, and actor. He designed Main Street USA, the submarine *Nautilus* for Disney's *20,000 Leagues Under the Sea*, the submarine *Proteus* for the film *Fantastic Voyage*, and the sets for such memorable films as *Sergeant York, Captain Blood*, and the Doris Day musical *Calamity Jane.*

In October, visit the Halloween Tree, a decorated oak tree located between the stockade gate and the Golden Horseshoe Saloon. Strung with lights and hand-painted jack-o'-lanterns, the tree was inspired by Ray Bradbury's 1972 fantasy novel *The Halloween Tree*. It was dedicated to Bradbury in a Halloween 2007 ceremony.

Walt and Mark Twain

Two signature attractions in Frontierland — the *Mark Twain* riverboat and Tom Sawyer Island — are tributes to one of Walt's boyhood idols, novelist Mark Twain

(Samuel L. Clemens). Twain had an enormous influence on the young Walt Disney, and the parallels between their lives are surprising.

Mark Twain died in 1910, when Walt was eight years old. Both Twain and Disney were avid readers, but undistinguished students, and neither finished high school. Both had fathers who were stern, unimaginative, practical-minded men who changed occupations frequently, and moved their families from town to town. Both had affectionate, fun-loving mothers who helped compensate for the fathers' emotional distance.

When Twain was nearly four years old, his family moved to the small Missouri town of Hannibal; when Walt was four, his family moved to the small Missouri town of Marceline. Both men were shaped by their small town experiences, and both drew upon those experiences when creating their art. Both grew up in conditions verging on poverty, yet neither felt deprived of life's necessities. Both learned their trades in Kansas City before setting off for California in search of wealth and fame. Both played a major role in shaping American attitudes and culture.

And here's another interesting parallel: In Chapter 10 of Twain's *Adventures of Huckleberry Finn*, there's a scene in which Huck (who has been hiding out on Jackson's Island with Jim the escaped slave) takes a rowboat to town, dresses up as a girl, and has a conversation with Mrs. Loftus, a lonely woman on the edge of town. As Mrs. Loftus and Huck trade gossip, she becomes suspicious and realizes that Huck is a boy disguised as a girl.

In *Walt Disney: An American Original*, biographer Bob Thomas tells this parallel story about Walt Disney and his mother, Flora: "One day Flora answered the front door to find a nicely dressed woman. Flora began to converse with her until she recognized some of her own clothes. The visitor was Walt in his mother's clothes, a wig and makeup."[2] It's not hard to imagine that young Walt, who was an actor at heart, might have gotten the idea for that prank by reading *Huckleberry Finn*.

Twain's tales of the adventures of Tom Sawyer and Huck Finn fired the imagination of young Walt Disney. One Twain scenario that appealed to Walt was the notion of having an entire island to play on. In Twain's tales, that island was Jackson's Island.

In Chapter 13 of *Adventures of Tom Sawyer*, Tom and his friends Joe Harper and Huck Finn take a raft to an uninhabited island. There they all take pirate names: Tom Sawyer, the Black Avenger of the Spanish Main, Huck Finn the Red-Handed, and Joe Harper the Terror of the Seas. They talk to each other in pirate speech: "Luff, and bring her to the wind!" "Aye-aye, sir!" "Send the r'yals up! Lay out aloft, there, half a dozen of ye!" "Aye-aye, sir!"

Young Walt was inspired by the dream of escaping to an island, beyond the reach of grown-ups and everyday life. Jackson's Island was where a boy could pretend and play and explore to his heart's content — a place where he could be anybody, from any time, in any place, living any adventure.

Fast-forward to 1954, as Walt was designing Disneyland. Art director Marvin Davis has helped to conceptualize and map out Main Street USA, Fantasyland, Frontierland, and Tom Sawyer Island. Though Walt loved Davis's designs for the rest of Disneyland, Davis's designs for the island did not match Walt's boyhood conception of Jackson's Island from the Twain novels.

Bob Thomas wrote, "Marv Davis had labored over the contours of Tom Sawyer Island, but his efforts failed to please Walt. 'Give me that thing,' Walt said. That night he worked for hours in his red-barn workshop. The next morning, he laid tracing paper on Davis's desk and said, 'Now that's the way it should be.' The island was built according to his design."[3]

The original Tom Sawyer Island was perhaps the most deeply personal expression of Walt's own boyhood dreams to be found anywhere in Disneyland. Tom Sawyer Island is the playground Walt wished he could have had as a boy. It's the only attraction in the Park that Walt himself drew up with his own hands, in his backyard barn on Carolwood Drive.

Lafitte's Tavern (formerly Harper's Mill)
on Tom Sawyer Island. (Photo: Boris Dzhingarov)[4]

Just as writers write the books they always wished they could read, Walt built the playground his inner child had always wanted to explore. Tom Sawyer Island was the tangible fulfillment of all his boyhood wishes.

Walt explained: "I put in all the things I wanted to do as a kid — and couldn't."[5]

On and around Tom Sawyer Island, young and old could relive the adventures of Tom Sawyer and Huckleberry Finn. The island was crisscrossed with trails, hidden tunnels, swinging rope bridges, and a few explorable landmarks such as Tom and Huck's Tree House, Injun Joe's Cave (now Dead Man's Grotto), Harper's Mill (now Lafitte's Tavern), and Fort Wilderness. But there were no mechanical thrill rides, no lines, no tickets to buy, no time limits, no rules. Walt wanted the experience to come from the imagination of his guests, not his Imagineers.

Walt dedicated Tom Sawyer Island in June 1956, a year after Disneyland officially opened. The event was celebrated with an old-fashioned catfish fry at the Plantation House restaurant (where New Orleans Square stands today). Two honored guests, Chris Winkler and Perva Lou Smith from Hannibal, Missouri, portrayed Tom Sawyer and Becky Thatcher. Winkler and Smith read a proclamation from the governor of Missouri (without any force of law) declaring Tom Sawyer Island to be annexed territory of the great state of Missouri.

More than fifty years later, on May 25, 2007, Disneyland reopened the island with a new theme and a new name: Pirate's Lair on Tom Sawyer Island. The reopening of the island coincided with the release of *Pirates of the Caribbean: At World's End*, the third installment of the Disney film series. The movie tie-in prompted some Disney fans to complain that the company had ruined Walt's original island in order to sell movie tickets — a repeat of the Tarzan's Treehouse miscue.

As a fan of Tom Sawyer Island, I'm conflicted. It's true — much of Walt's original vision for Tom Sawyer Island has been lost, probably forever. The most lamentable loss of all is Fort Wilderness. I loved exploring the island and Fort Wilderness as a boy. As a dad, I enjoyed sharing this frontier fort with my children. Now it's gone.

Fort Wilderness was made of genuine hand-hewn logs, and it seemed sturdy enough to stand forever. The theme of the attraction was the era of American expansion and the War of 1812, when the American flag had fifteen stars instead of fifty. Walt wanted Tom Sawyer Island to inform and inspire as well as entertain. Fort Wilderness was designed to teach young people about the era of Davy Crockett and Major General Andrew Jackson. The fort had a graveyard, block houses, parapets, stairs, a trading post, a regimental headquarters, and a rifle roost.

A raft passes Walt's Fort Wilderness, circa 1960.
(Photo: BeenAroundAWhile at en.wikipedia)[6]

In his dedication speech on opening day, Walt said, "Disneyland is dedicated to the ideals, the dreams, and the hard facts that have created America." Fort Wilderness embodied some of the "hard facts" of those early days of America's history, including the battles fought from other fortified parapets, and the graveyards where the fallen were laid to rest. Fort Wilderness was a feast for the imagination, but it was also a sobering reminder of America's turbulent past.

The best feature of Fort Wilderness was the secret tunnel. Yes, a *real* secret tunnel. You entered the tunnel through an unmarked door near the back of the fort. It led to a gap in the rocks which took you to a path along the river bank. The tunnel opening was narrow and forbidding for adults, but inviting for kids — and because it was unmarked, the tunnel conferred bragging rights on youngsters who knew it was there.

Fort Wilderness may have been, in part, a victim of global economic woes. The Walt Disney Company opened Disneyland Paris in 1992, just as the European economy was tanking. In its first three years of operation, Disneyland Paris lost hundreds of millions of dollars per year, forcing other Disney parks, including Disneyland, to tighten their belts.

As Werner Weiss observed at Yesterland.com, "In the mid-1990s, Disneyland management began to cut back on maintenance throughout the Park . . . at a time when much of Disneyland was reaching an age when it needed more maintenance, not less. . . . Perhaps the deterioration of Fort Wilderness was inevitable due to age, but perhaps it would have been avoidable with proper maintenance."[7]

What was the maintenance issue that led to the fort's deterioration? Termites. Walt's fort might have been saved by a timely pest inspection and fumigation — a maintenance issue that was possibly put off because Disneyland Paris was hemorrhaging cash at the time.

In early 2003, Disney launched a major renovation of Tom Sawyer Island which included draining and refilling the Rivers of America. When the island reopened in the summer, many of its features had been improved or reconstructed: the barrel (pontoon) bridge, the swaying suspension bridge, and more. The upgrade enhanced both the aesthetic appeal and the safety of the attraction.

But when guests rushed to revisit the Fort Wilderness stockade, they found the gates shut and barred. Walt's frontier playground — every kid's favorite fort — was locked tight, never to reopen.

From 2003 to 2007, *Fantasmic!* cast members used Fort Wilderness as a backstage costuming area for the nightly show. In 2007, the Disney Company demolished Walt's original Fort Wilderness and replaced the log fort with a structure made of milled lumber instead of hand-hewn logs. The new structure looks vaguely fort-like, but is not open to the public. It is reserved exclusively for the use of *Fantasmic!* cast members.

It was an ignominious ending for Fort Wilderness and for the nostalgic memories of countless Disneyland visitors over the decades. Walt would never have allowed the demise of Fort Wilderness on his watch.

But I don't think Walt would necessarily object to the pirate-themed makeover of Tom Sawyer Island. He always saw the island as having a pirate motif, and his original design for Tom Sawyer Island included a place called Pirate's Cove. Early promotional art for Tom Sawyer Island featured an image of Tom rafting toward the island, the mast of the raft flying a pirate flag with a skull-and-crossbones.

Today's pirate-themed Castle Rock on Tom Sawyer Island

Walt, who conceived and supervised the Pirates of the Caribbean attraction in New Orleans Square, enjoyed tales of swaggering buccaneers who piled up treasure in secret caves, and whose only law was "dead men tell no tales." His fascination with pirates can be traced, in part, to the influence of Mark Twain.

Did the Disney Company go too far in erasing Walt's original vision for Tom Sawyer Island? Maybe so. Much of what made the island so much fun to explore is simply gone. Yet remnants of Walt's original island remain. You can still climb Castle Rock for an unparalleled view of Frontierland and Critter Country. And Tom and Huck's Tree House remains largely unchanged, except for a few pirate-themed additions.

Pirates have always been part of the story of Tom Sawyer — the boy who called himself "the Black Avenger of the Spanish Main."

The Petrified Tree

Late in the afternoon of July 11, 1956, Walt and Lillian pulled up at the entrance to Pike Petrified Forest, a privately-owned tract of land strewn with petrified trees. The Disneys had been vacationing at the Broadmoor Hotel at Cheyenne Lake, Colorado.

Walt got out of the car, strode to the house next to the arched entrance, and knocked on the door. Lillian waited in the car. A boy named Toby Wells answered the door and Walt said he wanted to look around at the petrified trees. "It's getting dark," the boy said. "You won't see much. The tour costs thirty-five cents."

"That's fine," Walt said, handing over a quarter and a dime.

So Toby gave him a quick tour. Walt immediately took an interest in the petrified base of an ancient tree — a large, symmetrical fossil measuring seven feet in diameter and weighing five tons.

"I'd like to buy that one," Walt said.

The fossilized trees were not supposed to be for sale, the boy said, but he'd get the manager. "What's your name, mister?"

"I'm Walt Disney from Los Angeles."

The boy stared closely at Walt — and recognized the famous host of the *Disneyland* TV show. Then he shouted for the manager.

The manager of Pike Petrified Forest came out and agreed to sell the fossil to Walt for $1,650, and he agreed to supervise the shipment of the five-ton tree remnant to California. Walt wrote the man a check and signed the guestbook, then he and Lillian drove off.

This story, so far, is true.

But after Walt purchased the petrified tree, he began to tell a story about the fossil. He bought it, he said, as an anniversary gift for Lillian. Their thirty-first wedding anniversary was coming up in two days, on July 13. According to Walt, the petrified tree spent a year in Mrs. Disney's garden, then she tired of it and re-gifted it to Disneyland, where it was placed in Frontierland, near the Rivers of America.

The plaque on the fossilized tree states, "Presented by Mrs. Walt Disney, September, 1957." Walt's claim that he gave it to his wife as an anniversary present is confirmed by the plaque, and has been repeated on the official Disneyland blog, and in numerous Disney biographies (including *How to Be Like Walt*, the book I co-wrote in 2004 with Pat Williams).

But while researching this book, I learned that the fossil never spent a moment in Mrs. Disney's garden. A letter Walt wrote to the proprietor of Pike Petrified Forest, dated July 19, 1956, was released in 2009. It read in part:

> This will serve as a confirmation of your telephone conversation with my secretary, Dolores Voght, on July 18th, regarding the petrified stump. It is my understanding that you will deliver the stump direct to DISNEYLAND at Anaheim, California, within Thirty days. . . . We are enclosing a map showing the location of DISNEYLAND and we suggest you make delivery at the Warehouse Entrance which is on West Street.[8]

Disney historian Todd James Pierce exchanged emails with Diane Disney Miller, who explained:

> The whole thing has been embellished. . . . It became a family joke. He did buy that tree stump, and told her, and everyone else that it was his gift to her. Of course it went right to Disneyland. . . .
>
> The "gift to my wife" was just a gag. He was the consummate gag man, and proud of it.[9]

So Walt bought the fossilized tree not as an anniversary present, but to enhance Disneyland as an amusement park that educates as well as it entertains. The rest

of Walt's story is just a "tall tale," a time-honored tradition of the frontier.

The five-ton petrified tree in Disneyland is a fragment of a Sequoia redwood that probably stood about 200 feet tall, one of many such trees in a subtropical forest that covered the region millions of years ago. The sign on the petrified tree says it grew "55 to 70 million years ago in what is now Colorado." However, paleontologists at the Florissant Fossil Beds National Monument (which now encompasses the site where Walt purchased the tree) say that the petrified trees of that area are from the late Eocene era and are about 34 million years old.[10]

The petrified tree in Frontierland has much to teach us about the history of life on the earth — and about Walt Disney, consummate gag man and mythmaker.

Walt's Frontierland is still there, waiting to be explored and enjoyed. His riverboat still churns the Rivers of America. The Golden Horseshoe Saloon — one of Walt's favorite hang-outs in the Park — still serves up laughter and music along with fried chicken, chili, and ice cream sundaes. Though Tom Sawyer Island has changed, and much of it has vanished, much of Walt's island remains the same.

And the next time you get your picture taken beside Walt's petrified tree, you can say you know the legend — *and* you know what *really* happened.

CHAPTER SEVEN

Walt's New Orleans Square

"The Louisiana purchase was probably the greatest real estate deal of all time. It included all of the territory from the Gulf of Mexico to Canada. Total cost: eleven million dollars. By the way, Disneyland's New Orleans Square alone cost fifteen million — but of course, a dollar went much further in those days."
—*Walt Disney*

One quiet Sunday morning in the late 1950s, Walt and Herb Ryman were walking in Frontierland along New Orleans Street, talking about plans for a new themed land in the park. Walt called it "New Orleans Square." Attendance in the Park was light, so it was the kind of day when Walt could walk around without being mobbed or even recognized. As they walked, Walt pointed here and there, describing his vision for his new land.

Then, out of the corner of his eye, Ryman noticed four women approaching from behind Walt. One of the women tapped Walt on the shoulder and said, "Pardon me, but you're Walt Disney."

Ryman later said he expected Walt to be annoyed by the interruption — especially if they wanted autographs. But instead of being upset, Walt seemed pleased. He smiled broadly, took the hand of each lady, and said, "How are you?"

The woman who had spoken blushed and said, "You don't know me."

"Well, I do now."

"We wanted to know if you'd sign our book."

"I'd be delighted to." And to Herb Ryman's surprise, Walt signed autographs for each of the four ladies.[1]

I'm not sure why Herb Ryman was surprised, because Walt was always eager to talk to his guests and to make their stay a magical one. And Walt was always happiest when he was planning and building his next big project.

Frames from an 8mm home movie of Walt in Frontierland, 1955. He was already planning to carve New Orleans Square out of Frontierland at the time. (Photo: Antarctic96)[2]

Walt's New Land

Long before Disneyland opened in 1955, Walt knew he wanted to devote a section of the Park to a re-creation of old New Orleans. That's why there was a street in Frontierland called New Orleans Street. Aunt Jemima's Pancake House (later called Aunt Jemima's Kitchen, now the

River Belle Terrace) stood on New Orleans Street — a gleaming example of graceful French Quarter architecture just a few steps from the rugged, rustic atmosphere of Frontierland.

A little further down, on the waterfront side of New Orleans Street, was the Dixieland Bandstand. There the Disneyland Strawhatters quintet performed "Nawlins"-style jazz — from "When the Saints Go Marching In" to "Basin Street Blues." The Bandstand was removed in 1962.

These New Orleans-style touches in Frontierland reflected Walt's desire to have a New Orleans-themed land from the get-go. By the late 1950s, Walt's Imagineers had drawn up plans for a section of Frontierland that would include a haunted house, a walk-through pirate wax museum, a pirate-themed shop called Thieves Market, and an elegant restaurant called the Blue Bayou. Souvenir maps of Disneyland in 1958 labeled Frontierland's proposed new section "New Orleans Square," though it was not located where New Orleans Square stands today.

In the early 1960s, Walt committed his Imagineers to producing attractions for the 1964 New York World's Fair. This meant delaying work on the New Orleans-themed project in order to meet the deadline for the World's Fair attractions. This delay was a blessing in disguise. The World's Fair project unleashed a torrent of advances in Audio-Animatronics technology — lifelike figures that moved and talked.

After building such attractions as Great Moments with Mr. Lincoln, the Carousel of Progress, and "it's a small world" for the World's Fair, Walt and his Imagineers turned their attention once more to New Orleans Square. These powerful technologies opened up fantastic new vistas of entertainment and illusion. The old notion of a pirate wax museum filled with motionless statues seemed quaint and boring to Walt and his Imagineers. Why limit their imagination? If they could dream it, they could build it.

Walt decided to build a water-based dark ride with a reenactment of a pirate raid on a Caribbean fort, with a storyline, dialogue, soundtrack, motion, fire effects, and more. The result was Pirates of the Caribbean — one of two signature attractions of New Orleans Square (the other is The Haunted Mansion). Pirates of the Caribbean was the last attraction supervised by Walt himself.

New Orleans Square's Court of Angels. (Photo: HarshLight)[3]

New Orleans Square was the first new themed land added to Disneyland after the Park's opening. On July 24, 1966, Walt conducted the ceremony opening New Orleans Square to the public. Though Walt didn't feel well that day, he was as jovial as ever while presiding over the festivities. With him was Victor H. Schiro, the mayor of the City of New Orleans.

New Orleans Square covers about three acres and was built at a cost of $15 million — $4 million more (in unadjusted dollars) than the cost of the Louisiana Purchase, and just $2 million shy of the original (unadjusted) price tag for Disneyland, eleven years earlier.

The winding streets of New Orleans Square do not form a "square" in the conventional sense. The name is derived from Vieux Carré (French for "Old Square"), the original name for the French Quarter, the most historic neighborhood of the City of New Orleans.

When Walt worked with various corporations to build attractions for the 1964 New York World's Fair, he was often the guest of corporate leaders at private clubs and lounges for VIPs. He decided that Disneyland needed a private club, and he began planning an area in New Orleans Square for elite members and corporate sponsors. He assigned Emile Kuri — the Hollywood set designer who had decorated his apartment over the Fire House — to create a plush environment for the club.

The private club was named Club 33 because the original location of its entrance was at 33 Royal Street, next to the Blue Bayou Restaurant. (Some say the name may also derive from the thirty-three corporate sponsors of Disneyland in 1967.) The club opened on June 15, 1967, eleven months after New Orleans Square opened and six months after Walt's death. The club's existence was originally a secret, and the only outward clue to its location was an otherwise unmarked door with an address plate that read "33." In the New Orleans Square remodel of 2014, the entrance was moved to 33 Orleans Street, across from La Mascarade d'Orleans. Today, Club 33 is the worst-kept "secret" in Disneyland.

Membership confers an array of privileges, including fine dining in the dark paneled jazz lounge Le Salon Nouveau and the formal Le Grand Salon, admittance to 1901 (a private lounge in Disney California Adventure), a private balcony for viewing the *Fantasmic!* show, and more. Club 33 is, at present, the only establishment in the Park that serves alcohol.

The club features an antique-style glass elevator that Walt and his Imagineers built, based on an elevator in a Paris hotel where he and Lillian once stayed. Club 33 also contains a harpsichord (which has been played by such celebrities as Paul McCartney and Elton John), displays of antiques collected by Lillian Disney, a gallery of original artwork from *Fantasia* and other productions, and props from Disney films (such as a vintage glass phone booth from *The Happiest Millionaire* and a carved walnut table with marble top from *Mary Poppins*).

The cost of Club membership is not officially published, but is reported to include an initiation fee of at least $50,000 plus annual dues of $15,000 or more. Applicants can wait a dozen years or more for a membership to become available.

Pirates of the Caribbean

A major portion of what we now know as New Orleans Square once belonged to "the lost land of Disneyland," Holidayland. Opening on June 16, 1957, Holidayland was a nine-acre lawn and picnic ground with a baseball field, volleyball courts, sandboxes for horseshoes, slides and other playground equipment, food concessions, and a candy-striped circus tent. Holidayland could hold up to 7,000 people, had its own entrance into Disneyland, and could be booked for corporate events. Sometimes called "the least photographed land in the Park," Holidayland was closed in September of 1961 because it was under-utilized, and the space was needed for the show buildings for Pirates of the Caribbean and The Haunted Mansion.

The Bride Market scene in Pirates of the Caribbean. (Photo: HarshLight)[4]

Walt brought in his top animation and background artists to work on Pirates of the Caribbean. Claude Coats had created the colorful, evocative castle backgrounds in *Cinderella* and Gepetto's village in *Pinocchio*, as well as the stunning color-drenched Rainbow Caverns in Frontierland; Walt brought him aboard to create a believable, colorful Caribbean town for the pirates to ransack. Walt assigned veteran character animator Marc Davis to the task of transforming murderous pirates into drunken, lovable clowns — and Davis pulled it off with aplomb.

Marc's wife, Alice Davis, designed the costumes. Animator-turned-sculptor Blaine Gibson translated Davis's whimsical character sketches into lifelike molded latex figures.

Walt recruited legendary animator X Atencio to play an unusual role in the Pirates attraction. Born Francis Xavier Atencio, he started in 1938 as an apprentice Disney animator, making twelve dollars a week. He spent nearly three decades in feature animation. Then, in the early 1960s, Walt turned X Atencio's world upside-down.

"Walt had an uncanny knack for discovering talent," X said in an interview with Pat Williams. "He'd see talent in people that they didn't even see in themselves. I had been an animator all those years. One day Walt said, 'X, it's time for you to move.' And he sent me over to WED Enterprises, where they were building attractions for Disneyland.

"When I got there, I said, 'Walt sent me. What do you want me to do?' And nobody had a clue what I was supposed to do there. Walt hadn't told anyone. And I was there for a few days without any work to do.

"Finally, Walt called and said, 'X, I want you to write the script for Pirates of the Caribbean. There'll be scenes with pirates and townspeople and so forth, and I want you to write all the dialogue.' I had never scripted anything before, but Walt said, 'I know you can do this.' That's how I became a writer."

Atencio's script walked a fine line, turning the lusty, violent, R-rated lives of lawless pirates into family-friendly entertainment. A prime example is the scene where the pirate auctioneer offers a "winsome wench" for sale, adding, "Stout-hearted and corn-fed she be." A drunk pirate replies, "Hey! Be ya sellin' her by the pound?" The auctioneer tells her, "Shift yer cargo, dearie, show 'em your larboard side!"

While working on the script, X suggested to Walt that the attraction needed a pirate song to play throughout the ride. He suggested a melody and some lyrics, assuming that Walt would assign the songwriting chores to his top songwriters, the Sherman Brothers, who wrote the music for *Mary Poppins* and "it's a small world." But when Walt heard his ideas, he said, "Oh, this is good. If you need some help with the music, get George Bruns to score it."

So the first song X Atencio ever wrote became one of the best-known Disney songs of all time — "Yo Ho, Yo Ho, A Pirate's Life For Me." X also performed the voice of the talking skull at the waterfall drop of the ride, and went on to write the script and songs for The Haunted Mansion.

Walt personally supervised the creation of the attraction, and even acted out many of the characters for his artists (in the past, he had often acted out characters for his animated features, such as *Snow White and the Seven Dwarfs*). Walt knew exactly what he wanted, and he devoted himself to realizing his vision. He lavished $8 million on Pirates of the Caribbean, spending most of that vast sum on developing the 119 Audio-Animatronic figures (sixty-four people and fifty-five animals) that populate the attraction.

Disney Imagineer Yale Gracey created such realistic fire effects for the burning port city that the Anaheim Fire Department made Disney install an emergency shutoff to stop the fire effects in the event of a fire alarm. The fire chief worried that, in an emergency, the special effects might confuse his firefighters.

The attraction uses the same boat system Disney Imagineers successfully employed in "it's a small world." The façade of Pirates of the Caribbean was inspired by The Cabildo, the seat of Louisiana's government during French and Spanish colonial days, and the building where the Louisiana Purchase documents were signed.

As construction of the Pirates attraction proceeded, Walt and his creative team conducted a dry run. To create the illusion of cruising through the attraction in a boat, Imagineers wheeled Walt through the attraction on a camera dolly. X Atencio walked through the attraction as Walt rode through, and X was dismayed to hear the lines of his script clashing with each other. Over here, Carlos the town magistrate begged for his life. Over there, the Auctioneer bartered pirate brides. Further down, a pirate named Old Bill offered a tot of rum to a couple of stray cats. It was impossible to hear all the lines clearly and get the entire story.

X expected Walt to hate it. He began to apologize for writing too much dialogue — but Walt stopped him. "I love it!" Walt said. "It's like a cocktail party. People come to cocktail parties, and they tune in a conversation over here, then a conversation over there. Each time the guests come through here, they'll hear something else. That'll bring them back time and again."[5]

This is one of the keys to the attraction's enduring appeal. It's so richly detailed in both sights and sounds that you simply can't absorb it all in one visit. Every time you experience Pirates of the Caribbean, you discover details you never noticed before — including many that have been there since the beginning.

During the late stages of construction of the Pirates attraction, Walt talked to some construction crewmen and discovered that one of them came from the bayou country of Louisiana. Walt always enjoyed gathering impressions and ideas from everyday people, so he took the construction worker for a walk through the bayou section at the beginning of the attraction.

"What do you think?" Walt asked at the end of their stroll. "Is it realistic? Does it remind you of the bayou where you grew up?"

"It's good," the man replied, "but something's missing. Can I walk through it again?"

So Walt and the construction worker walked through a second time. They reached the shack in the swamp where an old man sits in his rocking chair — and the worker snapped his fingers. "Fireflies," he said. "There aren't any fireflies in this swamp."

A few days later, electric fireflies shed their soft glow over Walt's bayou.

It has been said that Walt imagined the Pirates of the Caribbean attraction but never got to experience it. Not true. He got to ride the attraction on July 24, 1966, the same day he officially opened New Orleans Square. He was hoping to open the Pirates attraction within a few days, but after riding through it that one-and-only time, he ordered it closed until changes could be made.

Ben Harris, then a Disneyland cast member, was present when Walt stepped out of the boat, and he recalls that Walt had filled a page with notes on changes he wanted made. Less than six months later, Walt passed away — and his Imagineers honored his memory by carrying out his instructions to the letter.[6]

Peggy Matthews Rose told me about an incident that took place on or about that same day. "My brother, John

Matthews," she said, "was working in the character program at the Park in 1966. He played Mickey, the White
Rabbit, and Thumper." (Peggy started working in the
Disneyland character program on December 23, 1967, a
year after Walt died.)

"John came home fuming one day," she recalled. "He
was upset because Walt had laid off all the workers who
had been hired for the Blue Bayou restaurant. Walt had
done a Pirates and Blue Bayou walkthrough that day,
then he had put the opening off for about a year. The restaurant and the Pirates ride are joined together in the
bayou section, so the restaurant couldn't open until the
attraction was completed. Walt wouldn't approve the attraction until some lighting problems and other issues
were fixed and everything was just-so. Pirates of the Caribbean opened late, but when it opened, it was perfect.
Walt always knew what he wanted. That's why the attraction is as popular today as it ever was."

Pat Williams interviewed Disney legend Thurl Ravenscroft, who recalled, "Walt dreamed up the Pirates of
the Caribbean attraction. He told his artists what he
wanted it to look like, and they drew up the plans and
constructed a scale model. One day, Walt walked me
through the model and showed me where everything

would be — the waterfall, the pirate ship, the burning town. He had dreamed it in exact detail, and he was excited to watch it take shape."

Walt dreamed it — but he didn't live to see it opened. Pirates of the Caribbean opened on March 18, 1967, three months after Walt's death. Actress Dorothy Lamour christened the attraction, smashing a bottle of Mississippi River water over the anchor near the entrance.

The anchor is said to have come from a ship captained by legendary pirate Jean Lafitte during the Battle of New Orleans, January 1815. (Recruited by Major General Andrew Jackson, Lafitte fought on the side of America against the British.)

More than a third of a billion people have passed through Pirates of the Caribbean since it opened. It's the most popular attraction at Disneyland — or at any theme park in the world.

The Disneyland Dream Suite

To the west of the entrance to The Pirates of the Caribbean, you'll see an ornate wrought-iron balcony with the gilded initials WD and RD (for Walt Disney and Roy Disney). That balcony, which shades a quick-service gumbo restaurant called Royal Street Veranda, is part of Walt's Royal Suite, which is now known as The Disneyland Dream Suite.

While Walt was building New Orleans Square in the early 1960s, he realized he needed a large suite of rooms for entertaining corporate leaders and other VIPs. Walt's Fire House apartment just wasn't big enough or quiet enough for entertaining — the Main Street crowd noise, musical soundtrack, parades, and band concerts were not conducive to business meetings during Park hours.

So Walt selected a more quiet and out-of-the-way location for the place he called The Royal Suite, above the façade building for Pirates of the Caribbean. He hired Dorothea Redmond, the set designer for *Gone with the Wind* and several Hitchcock films, to create the layout, and he had his wife Lillian and set decorator Emile Kuri decorate the suite in grand French Provincial style.

The Royal Suite was nearly completed when Walt Disney died in mid-December 1966. Walt's brother Roy halted work on the suite, saying that the Disney family would not be able to enjoy the place without Walt.

During the late 1970s and early '80s, Disneyland International used the suite as a planning office for Tokyo Disneyland. From 1987 to 2007, the space housed The Disney Gallery, a combined museum and merchandise shop displaying original Imagineering artwork used in designing Disneyland. In 2007, The Disney Gallery moved to Main Street and the Suite was converted into the Disneyland Dream Suite, laid out and decorated according to the original designs of Dorothea Redmond and Emile Kuri.

Overnight stays in The Disneyland Dream Suite are given out as prizes in Disneyland promotions, and the Suite also hosts VIP guests. It is decorated according to Walt's original wishes, with some added touches that Walt would certainly appreciate: a carousel horse, paintings of European castles, a mechanical songbird, a patio illuminated with Chinese lanterns and fireflies, and a model train that runs around a high display ledge.

The Disneyland Dream Suite more than fulfills Walt's vision for The Royal Suite. Very few people are privileged to visit the Dream Suite, yet it is a quintessential part of Walt's Disneyland.

The Haunted Mansion

Though the Haunted Mansion was not opened until two and a half years after Walt's death, a haunted house was one of the earliest ideas Walt had for his Park. In 1951, when Walt planned to build Mickey Mouse Park near the Burbank studio, he assigned conceptual artist Harper Goff to prepare drawings of a proposed walk-through attraction he called a "ghost house."

In 1953, Walt assigned art director Marvin Davis to the "ghost house" project. Davis created designs for a forbidding "house on the hill," a dark and brooding Victorian mansion that would look down on Main Street.

In 1957, art director Ken Anderson created a drawing of an elegant but run-down Victorian-style mansion with elaborate wrought-iron grillwork, situated in a damp, mossy bayou. Walt rejected Anderson's concept because he wanted nothing in Disneyland to look dilapidated or unkempt. Everything had to be well-maintained. He told his designers, "We'll take care of the outside and let the ghosts take care of the inside." That's the secret to the allure of the Haunted Mansion.

Walt had visited Winchester Mystery House in San Jose, California, and loved the idea of a mansion filled with hallways and stairs that seemed to lead nowhere, rooms that hid mysteries and legends, and illusions that boggled the senses. The Mystery House is no rundown hovel — it's a Queen Anne-style Victorian mansion, well-maintained in a beautifully landscaped setting. That's what Walt wanted his Haunted Mansion to be.

Ken Anderson went back to the drawing board and produced drawings of an eerie but immaculate Victorian mansion on a well-kept New Orleans street. Anderson called it Bloodmere Manor. Walt took one look and instantly okayed it.

The Haunted Mansion façade was constructed in 1963, three years before the New Orleans Square opening in July 1966. Yet the Mansion remained a façade, not an attraction, for six years. Its gates were locked tight. I remember peering through the Mansion fence as a boy and wondering why Disneyland had a haunted house you couldn't enter. Finally, on August 9, 1969, The Haunted Mansion opened for business.

Walt had originally envisioned The Haunted Mansion as a walk-through attraction. In 1961, flyers handed out at Disneyland's main entrance announced that The Haunted Mansion would open in 1963. But the Mansion's show building remained empty while Imagineers focused on creating attractions for the 1964 New York World's Fair.

In a 1965 episode of Walt Disney's *Wonderful World of Color*, Walt gave viewers a tour of WED Enterprises, his Imagineering company. He talked about future projects, including The Haunted Mansion. Marc Davis displayed his painting of a beautiful woman who morphs into the hideous Medusa. Imagineer Rolly Crump described a feature called the Museum of the Weird — a collection of oddities that included a chair that stands up and talks, a melting candle man, statues that follow you with their eyes, and other unsettling illusions. The Museum of the Weird did not materialize, but some of its illusions are part of today's Haunted Mansion.

The Haunted Mansion in 1971. (Photo: Lee Denney)

The illusions of The Haunted Mansion were largely the work of Imagineers Rolly Crump and Yale Gracey, who worked as a team. Walt gave Crump and Gracey an entire warehouse at the Burbank studio to haunt as their ghost factory. They immersed themselves in influences ranging from the avant-garde films of Jean Cocteau and Federico Fellini to a 1913 book, *The Boy Mechanic: 700 Things for Boys to Do* by Popular Mechanics.

Crump reveled in the freedom Walt gave him to stretch his imagination. Walt didn't care about deadlines or bottom lines. Crump and Gracey were engineering wonders in that warehouse, and Walt gave them a free hand. "Working for WED in the 1950s and '60s was heaven until Walt passed," Crump said. "Things really changed after that."

After Walt's death, Crump and Gracey were caught in a crossfire between Disney brass and WED Enterprises executives who had conflicting notions of what the Haunted Mansion should be. Some said the Mansion should be stocked with thrills and chills, others thought it should provoke laughter instead of screams. Those who controlled the budget and made decisions after Walt's death couldn't understand Rolly Crump's unique approach — which Walt loved — of combining spookiness with Disney-style foolery in the same attraction.

Crump once told a story about his days in the Haunted Mansion department of WED Enterprises. He and Yale Gracey had a vast room filled with ghosts and magical devices and illusions spread all around. At the end of every workday, they would turn out the lights and go home. Sometime during the night, the janitors would come in to sweep the floors, empty the wastepaper baskets — and, to the dismay of Crump and Gracey, clean up the cobwebs the Imagineers had meticulously arranged on their creations. On one occasion, the Disney Personnel Department called Crump and asked that he and Gracey leave the lights on when they left. It seemed the janitors were creeped out by the Audio-Animatronic ghosts and monsters.

So Rolly Crump and Yale Gracey complied — sort of. They installed motion sensors that, when triggered, would turn the lights out and start all the ghost effects at the same time. The next morning, when Crump and Gracey arrived for work, they found all the spooky contraptions still running — and an abandoned push broom in the middle of the floor. Personnel called later that morning and told Crump the janitorial crew refused to go back to that room.

Was it just a mean-spirited prank? No. It was a test. Crump and Gracey wanted to know if their illusions and effects were realistically scary. Answer: Oh, yes.[7]

In the early development of the Mansion, when it was still envisioned as a walk-through, Imagineers viewed the attraction through the lens of a backstory that went like this:

A grim-faced butler greets a group of guests and escorts them through the Mansion, telling them the story of the late owner — a wealthy sea trader who built the many-roomed house for his bride. When the pretty young bride learned of her husband's secret past as a murderous pirate, she tried to leave him — so he killed her in a possessive rage. But she came back as a ghost to haunt him, driving him to madness and suicide. Having set the scene with this tragic tale, the butler would then conduct his guests on a fright-filled walking tour of the late sea trader's Mansion.

Though the backstory was later abandoned, hints of the tale can be seen to this day — the sailing ship weather vane that tops the Mansion, the sailing ship painting in the portrait hall, the hanged man suspended from the ceiling of the stretching room, and — in the attic of the Mansion — the haunting bride with her red glowing heart.

Drenched in Mystery and Magic

After Walt's death in December 1966, the Imagineering team arrived at a final configuration for the Haunted Mansion. Increasing attendance at the Park made it clear that a walk-through attraction was no longer feasible. A walk-through simply wouldn't move enough people fast enough. So the Imagineers adapted the Omnimover ride system from Tomorrowland's (now defunct) Adventure Thru Inner Space. They renamed the Omnimover vehicles "Doom Buggies." The Buggies could be controlled and turned to direct the riders' attention to various scenes in the show.

The ride was designed to guide you to a "stretching room" which not only introduces you to the attraction, but also transports you underground. The room fools the senses — you think the ceiling is rising, but in fact the floor is sinking. You are taking an elevator down to the portrait hall. As you walk along the portrait hall, you are walking along a tunnel that leads you underneath the Disneyland Railroad tracks. The tunnel takes you into a 37,000 square-foot show building. There, you step onto a Doom Buggy which transports you through the show building. Guests never realize that they have been outside the perimeter of the Park.

The song "Grim Grinning Ghosts" (written by X Atencio and scored by Buddy Baker) is woven throughout the attraction. Thurl Ravenscroft portrays one of the five singing busts in the graveyard. Paul Frees provides the haunting voice of the Ghost Host, who welcomes guests to the Mansion. (Frees also narrated the film shown at Great Moments with Mr. Lincoln, voiced most of the Pirates of the Caribbean characters, and supplied the voice for cartoon character Ludwig von Drake). The pipe organ played by a ghost in the ballroom is the same organ Captain Nemo played in Disney's *20,000 Leagues Under the Sea* (1954).

One of the most memorable illusions in the Haunted Mansion is the image of Madam Leota, the disembodied woman who speaks from the crystal ball. She is portrayed by Leota Toombs, a Disney Imagineer who worked in the Dimensional Design Department. The spectral voice of Madam Leota is provided by Eleanor Audley, who voiced the wicked stepmother in the 1950 animated feature *Cinderella*.

A seasonal overlay of the Haunted Mansion, called Haunted Mansion Holiday, premiered in 2001 and runs every year from mid-September through early January. Based on Tim Burton's motion picture *The Nightmare Before Christmas*, it features Leota Toombs' daughter, Kim Irvine, in the Madam Leota role and Corey Burton (replacing the late Paul Frees) as the Ghost Host.

Much of the Haunted Mansion was conceived after Walt's passing, though many individual elements of the attraction were in the works during Walt's lifetime. The beautiful, well-kept, stately exterior of the Mansion is pure Walt. And many of the frightening effects and baffling illusions of The Haunted Mansion would never have been invented if Walt had not given his Imagineers the freedom to attempt the impossible.

The Haunted Mansion is unique in that it's the only place Disneyland cast members are forbidden to smile, but are required to maintain a funereal demeanor. It's a great place to go for a spooky good time — and it's an authentic part of Walt's Disneyland. Walt Disney didn't envision the Mansion as a dark ride with people-moving Doom Buggies. But the notion of a haunted house in Disneyland, neat and pretty on the outside while haunted and scary (and hilariously funny) on the inside, was Walt's idea from the start.

Though short wait times in Disneyland are always welcome, Walt's Imagineers made sure you had plenty to see and enjoy when lines are long. The next time you visit the Haunted Mansion, take a few moments to read the inscriptions on the pet cemetery tombstones.

Everywhere you look in New Orleans Square, you see color, excitement, and beautiful antebellum architecture, all drenched in mystery and magic. Every lace-iron balcony, every lamppost, every hanging flower basket, and every string of lights or Mardi Gras beads sprang from the heart and soul of Walt Disney.

At the New Orleans Square Railroad Station, listen for the clicking telegraph message. Those clicks transmit a phrase from Walt's opening day speech of July 17, 1955: "To all who come to Disneyland, welcome. Here age relives fond memories of the past, and here youth may savor the challenge and promise of the future."

In the late 1990s, the recording of that Morse code message became damaged. George Eldridge, a ham radio operator, noticed that the message was a phrase fragment repeated on an endless loop. He contacted Disney media engineer Glenn Barker. With Eldridge's help, Barker was able to repair the audio recording, restoring a small but important feature of Walt's Disneyland.

The New Orleans Square Telegraph Office

Other hidden features of New Orleans Square that might interest you: In a shop called Le Bat en Rouge, near the Blue Bayou Restaurant, you'll find a witch in a cage. Turn the key of the cage and the witch will plead with you to set her free. Whatever you do, don't let the witch out of the cage.

Also near the Blue Bayou, pause in the street and listen to the sounds coming from the second story windows. You may hear a woman begging her songbirds *not* to sing the song from The Enchanted Tiki Room.

New Orleans Square is exclusive to Disneyland — you won't find it at any other Disney theme park. It's a whistle stop for the Disneyland Railroad, and home to the popular Mint Julep Bar, the Blue Bayou Restaurant (a fine dining establishment), and Café Orleans (where Lillian Disney's own espresso machine adorns the back wall). Above all, New Orleans Square is the setting for two of the most exciting, immersive dark ride experiences in Disneyland, Pirates of the Caribbean and The Haunted Mansion.

Walt's New Orleans Square is a clean, colorful, idealized New Orleans, a place where you can survive a pirate raid, invade the haunt of 999 ghosts, then enjoy a relaxing meal beside the Rivers of America. It was the last land Walt personally created — and one of his best.

CHAPTER EIGHT

Walt's Fantasyland

"Fantasyland is dedicated to the young and the young at heart, to those who believe that when you wish upon a star your dreams do come true."
—Walt Disney

Cross the drawbridge, then walk through Sleeping Beauty Castle, and you're there — Fantasyland. Walt's realm of pure imagination is bordered on the south by the Castle, on the east by the slopes of the Matterhorn, on the northeast by "it's a small world," and on the northwest by the Casey Jr. Circus Train.

But Fantasyland wasn't always as magical as it is today. Technical problems abounded during construction. Take, for example, the Dumbo Flying Elephants. They were built at Disney's Burbank studios, then shipped to Anaheim and attached to the ride mechanism. When engineers tested the ride, the elephants went 'round and 'round but were too heavy to fly. More powerful motors had to be installed, forcing the attraction to open a month late on August 16, 1955.

Another troubled attraction was the Casey Jr. Circus Train, also inspired by *Dumbo*. Originally planned as a roller coaster, the ride was supposed to careen up and down steep hills and through tight turns, giving young and old alike a circus-themed thrill ride. In test runs, however, the little engine puffed uphill saying "I think I can, I think I can" — only to stall and roll backwards. So much for positive thinking.

Imagineers pulled up the track, re-graded the hills, and transformed the "thrill ride" into a gentle excursion around Story Book Land. Even without thrills, Casey Jr. has been a crowd favorite after opening two weeks late, July 31, 1955.

Sleeping Beauty Castle. (Photo: Carterhawk)[1]

On opening day, Fantasyland offered six attractions —King Arthur Carrousel, Peter Pan Flight, Mr. Toad's Wild Ride, Snow White's Adventures, the Mad Tea Party, and Canal Boats of the World. Guests purchased tickets for each ride from ticket booths around the Park.

Rides were priced from 10 to 35 cents (Value Books with A through C coupons were introduced in October 1955).

In 1982, Disneyland stopped charging for each ride and removed most of the ticket booths. Four original booths remain, all in Fantasyland: the giant mushroom near Alice in Wonderland, the red-and-white lighthouse next to the Storybook Land Canal Boats, the pink-roofed train depot at the Casey Jr. Circus Train, and another booth that once stood in the middle of Fantasyland, now located near "it's a small world." These former ticket booths are reminders of Walt's Fantasyland of the 1950s.

Gateway to Fantasy

The gateway to Fantasyland is Sleeping Beauty Castle. While Disneyland was being planned and built, it was known variously as The Medieval Castle, Fantasyland Castle, and Robin Hood Castle, after Disney's 1952 live-action film *The Story of Robin Hood and His Merrie Men*. In a December 1954 episode of the *Disneyland* TV show, Walt referred to it as Snow White's Castle.[2] Finally, Walt decided to name his fantasy Castle after the heroine of his forthcoming motion picture.

While Walt was building Disneyland, he was also producing *Sleeping Beauty*, the animated feature many film critics say has never been surpassed. Based on the fairy tale by Charles Perrault, with a score based on Tchaikovsky's *Sleeping Beauty* ballet, it was Walt's first motion picture in stereophonic sound since *Fantasia*.

In mid-1954, Walt was simultaneously overseeing a major animated feature *and* the construction of Disneyland. The Burbank studio and the Anaheim construction site were about an hour apart by freeway. Unwilling to spend his days commuting, Walt practically lived at the Park.

Ironically, Walt's long absences from the studio benefited the artistry of *Sleeping Beauty*. When an animator completed a sequence for the film, he or she had to wait weeks for Walt to come and personally okay it. To keep busy, animators lavished hours of extra attention on their drawings — and the animation in *Sleeping Beauty* was raised to a level seldom seen before or since.[3]

While Walt's artists constructed castles out of ink and paint in Burbank, Walt built his Castle out of steel and stone in Anaheim. Inspired by the nineteenth century Neuschwanstein Castle in Bavaria, Sleeping Beauty Castle includes architectural touches from other sources. One unexpected detail is the Viollet-le-Duc Spire, to the right of the tallest tower as you face the drawbridge side. It's named for French Gothic Revival architect Eugène Viollet-le-Duc (1814-1879).

The spire goes unnoticed by most visitors — but writer Ray Bradbury noticed. Bradbury became acquainted with Imagineer John Hench while working on Spaceship Earth, the geodesic sphere attraction at Florida's Walt Disney World. After a vacation in Paris, Bradbury visited Disneyland — then he went home and called Hench.

Bradbury later recalled that conversation: "I said, 'I just noticed something about Sleeping Beauty Castle. There's a spire there that I saw last on top of Notre Dame and the Palais de Justice in Paris. How long has that been there on Sleeping Beauty's Castle?' [Hench] said, 'Twenty years.' I said, 'Who put it there?' He said, 'Walt did.' I said, 'Why?' 'Because he loved it.' I said, 'Ah! That's why I love Walt Disney. It cost a hundred thousand dollars to build a spire you didn't need, eh?' The secret of

Disney is doing things you don't need and doing them well, and then you realize you needed them all along."4

The Castle with a close-up of the Viollet-le-Duc Spire.
(Photo: SolarSurfer)

The Castle was designed by Herb Ryman, who produced the first drawing of Disneyland in 1953. Though the Castle is only seventy-seven feet tall, Ryman used forced perspective — using larger design elements at ground level and increasingly smaller design elements at higher levels — to make it seem taller than it is.

At Walt's insistence, the spires of Sleeping Beauty Castle are clad in genuine 22-karat gold leaf. Walt's brother Roy opposed gilding the spires as a needless expense, so Walt waited until Roy was out of the country, then he had the spires covered in gold.[5]

Jim Korkis observes that, thanks to the *Disneyland* TV show, Sleeping Beauty Castle became as much a symbol of Walt and the Disney Company as Mickey Mouse had been. But during the opening day broadcast, *Dateline: Disney*, the Castle became a major cause for alarm. At one point, live TV cameras showed *people* standing on the Castle parapet, waving to the crowd below. Some Disneyland visitors had invaded Walt's Castle through an unlocked door.

In 1955, the Castle interior consisted of scaffolding, ladders, and construction platforms — a dangerous place for unwary visitors. Disneyland executive Van Arsdale France located finance director Larry Tyson, and together they cleared the people out of the Castle.

When Walt learned of the intrusion, he had an idea. Clearly, people *wanted* to see the inside the Castle. So Walt took Imagineer Ken Anderson and decorator Emile Kuri into the Castle. There they found scores of feral cats — and they were attacked by swarms of fleas.

Walt ordered the cats be removed and placed with families. Then he fumigated the Castle and eliminated the flea infestation. Weeks later, Walt, Ken, and Emile finally quit itching and scratching.

Out of that horrible experience came a new attraction. Walt commissioned Ken Anderson to create a diorama of scenes from Walt's unfinished masterpiece, *Sleeping Beauty*. Though Disneyland opened in 1955, the movie would not premiere until 1959. In the meantime, Anderson's diorama would explain the tale of *Sleeping Beauty* to Fantasyland visitors.[6]

On April 29, 1957, almost two years before the release of *Sleeping Beauty*, Walt and actress Shirley Temple unveiled the Sleeping Beauty Diorama, a walk-through attraction in the Castle. Twenty-nine-year-old Temple was dressed as a princess in a red velvet cloak with a golden crown. With her three children beside her, she told the audience the story of *Sleeping Beauty*. Then she cut the ribbon and took her children into the attraction. Minutes later, she and her children emerged on an upper balcony and waved.

In those days, guests paid 10 cents (or an A coupon) to walk through the Sleeping Beauty Diorama. It featured eleven scenes adapted by Ken Anderson from the artwork of Eyvind Earle, production designer for the film.

The diorama was heavily revised in 1977, and some Disney purists dismissed it as a "Barbie and Ken" version of *Sleeping Beauty*. In 2008, Imagineers returned to Anderson's original artwork for inspiration while incorporating more three-dimensional figures, motion, and lighting effects. The 2008 version is probably closer to Walt's vision than the 1977 version, because it conveys the dark and brooding beauty of Eyvind Earle's designs.

Sleeping Beauty Castle is one of the most photographed landmarks in the world. Disney director James Algar recalled a story about the Castle from Disneyland's early days. The Park's head groundskeeper took Walt to a spot facing the Castle and said, "I need a fence and a sign here that says, 'Keep off the grass.' People trample the flowers to get a picture."

Walt said, "We don't need a fence. We need a walkway and a sign that says, 'Best Place to Photograph the Castle.' "[7] Walt listened to his guests. His solution was to make it *easier* to get a picture, not harder.

As you pass through the Castle into Fantasyland, notice the "golden spike" in the pavement. It's mistakenly rumored to be the geographical center of Disneyland. In fact, the center of Disneyland (before the addition of Mickey's Toontown) was the Central Plaza, where the "Partners" statue stands. Surveyors used the "spike" to align the Castle and drawbridge with Main Street.

In June or July 1965, a golden coat of arms was placed over the Castle entrance. It depicts three lions "passant in pale" (that is, the lions are walking and arranged in a vertical row). This is the Disney family coat of arms, dating back to Walt's ancestors who lived in Isigny-sur-Mer on the Normandy coast in France. The Disney family name was originally d'Isigny, meaning "of Isigny."

Some researchers claim the coat of arms on the Castle has no significance, and the actual Disney coat of arms consists of three fleur de lis. But the same three-lion image appears on the fountain in the Disneyland Dream Suite courtyard and on the Cinderella Castle in Florida's Magic Kingdom. Walt himself probably directed that the coat of arms be added to Sleeping Beauty Castle. He knew his family history well. According to the 1828 *Encyclopaedia Heraldica*, the Disney coat of arms consists of "three lions, passant, in pale," as shown on the Castle.[8]

On the east side of the Castle is Snow White Grotto, featuring statues of Snow White and the Seven Dwarfs beside a cascading waterfall. The grotto, which opened April 9, 1961, also serves as a wishing well. Disney donates coins from the grotto to children's charities.

In 1960 or '61, Walt received a package containing statues of Snow White and the Seven Dwarfs, carved by an Italian artist and donated anonymously to Disneyland. Walt wanted to incorporate them into the Park, but the artist had carved Snow White at the same height as the dwarfs. In the film, she's significantly taller.

John Hench solved the problem, using forced perspective to make Snow White appear farther away than the dwarfs. Adriana Caselotti, the voice of Snow White, made a new stereophonic recording of "I'm Wishing" from the film. When Snow White sings from the waterfall, her voice echoes from the well.

Jingles and Company

Emerging from the Castle, you see the King Arthur Carrousel — one of Walt's favorite attractions. He often said that Disneyland was inspired by weekend "Daddy's days" when he took his daughters to the merry-go-round at Griffith Park. As they rode around and around, he sat on a bench and imagined a park of his own.

And yes, the correct spelling is "Carrousel" with two R's. It's from the French *carrousel* ("jousting tournament") by way of the Spanish *carosella* ("little war"). King Arthur's Carrousel is a jousting-themed attraction, not circus-themed like most merry-go-rounds.

The King Arthur Carrousel was handcrafted by the Dentzel Carousel Company and was located at Sunnyside Beach Park in Toronto, Canada, from 1922 to 1954. Disney bought it and shipped it to California, where Imagineers refurbished it and replaced its menagerie of giraffes, lions, and zebras with horses. Disney purchased carved horses from other carousels across the country, including New York's Coney Island.

On opening day, the seventy-two Carrousel horses were painted brown, gray, or tan — except for a single white horse. That one white horse proved so popular that, in 1975, all the horses were painted white with distinctive color schemes for saddles and bridles. Each horse is individually named, and a list of the Carrousel horses is available at City Hall.

The Carrousel was moved about a hundred feet back from the Castle during a major Fantasyland rehab in 1983. This move enlarged the courtyard between the Castle and the Carrousel, improving crowd flow into Fantasyland. During a renovation in 2003, Imagineers replaced the Carrousel's turntable and added a ramp and a wheelchair-accessible bench to make the attraction ADA-compliant.

Walt's favorite horse, Jingles, is the lead horse on the Carrousel. You can spot Jingles easily — it's the outside horse located immediately after the bench.

In 2008, Jingles received a "Mary Poppins" makeover and was dedicated with actress Julie Andrews present. The jingle bells were painted gold. An escutcheon was painted on the saddle featuring silhouetted boots and a perched bird, an image of Mary Poppins flying with her umbrella, and the initials JA for Julie Andrews. The number 50 was added, symbolizing Disneyland's fiftieth anniversary in 2005, when Miss Andrews was Disneyland's special ambassador. Look for the "Hidden Mickey" of three jewels and the blue Mary Poppins umbrella on the saddle blanket.

An ornate Wurlitzer No. 157 Band Organ lends nostalgic charm to the Carrousel. The musical playlist consists mostly of themes from Walt's animated features and cartoons — "Minnie's Yoo Hoo" (which Walt co-wrote with Carl Stallings for *Mickey's Follies* in 1929), "Dumbo's Theme," "Baby Mine," "Casey Jr.," "Donald's Theme," "Who's Afraid of the Big Bad Wolf," and more.

The Most Popular Attraction in Fantasyland

When Walt was eight or nine, he and his brother Roy broke into their piggy banks to buy tickets for a road performance of James Barrie's *Peter Pan; or, The Boy Who Wouldn't Grow Up*. The play featured Broadway star Maude Adams in the title role. Walt's hometown, Marceline, Missouri, was a whistle-stop between St. Louis and Kansas City, and the Marceline show was for one night only.

Maude Adams toured in a private railroad car called *Tinkerbell*. A radiant performer, she cast her spell on young Walt. "For two hours," he said, "we lived in Never Land with Peter and his friends. I took many memories away from the theater with me, but the most thrilling of all was the vision of Peter flying through the air."

Walt and Roy put on their own version of *Peter Pan* at their elementary school. Roy manned the pulley and Walt swung on a rope. Walt later said, "It gave way, and I flew right into the faces of the surprised audience."[9]

In 1939, Walt acquired the film rights to *Peter Pan* from the Great Ormond Street Hospital in London for

5,000 British pounds (James Barrie had assigned the hospital all rights to the play in 1929).

In 1940, Walt contacted Miss Adams, inviting her to work with him on the project. She declined. Walt wrote in a letter to Disney executive Kay Kamen, "[Miss Adams said] the Peter whom she created was to her real life and blood, while another's creation of this character would only be a ghost to her. . . . Miss Adams is simply living in the past."[10]

Walt suspended work on *Peter Pan* during World War II, but by 1950, production was again in full swing. The studio filmed all the scenes using actors as reference models for the animators. Walt cast thirteen-year-old Kathryn Beaumont as Wendy Darling. Studio technicians sent her soaring with cables and pulleys.

Pat Williams interviewed Miss Beaumont. They met, along with Peggy Matthews Rose, at one of Walt's favorite restaurants, the Tam O'Shanter in Glendale. Miss Beaumont recalled being flown about the Burbank studio: "Most kids would say, 'What fun!' But I was nervous! I was hoisted up in the air in a harness and I was thinking that the floor of the stage looked so far down."

Why did Walt go to the trouble of filming *Peter Pan* in live action before proceeding to animate it? Because he wanted *Peter Pan* to be believable. He wanted his audience to *believe* that boys and girls could fly. Walt understood that, no matter how imaginative and fantastic your story might be, you must keep it grounded in reality if you want to be believed.[11] He once said, "When we do fantasy, we must not lose sight of reality."[12]

Peter Pan was released on February 5, 1953, at a cost of $4 million. The film earned $14 million in its initial run, and more than $87 million in subsequent releases.

Like Peter himself, the movie never ages — and neither does Peter Pan's Flight, the attraction based on the movie. It always has the longest lines in Fantasyland.

(A tip: While waiting in line for your flight to Never Land, listen for the voices of Peter and Wendy from the upper window to the right of the clock tower.)

Maude Adams died at her summer home in Tannersville, New York, on July 17, 1953, five months after the London premiere of *Peter Pan*, and exactly two years before Peter Pan's Flight debuted. She was eighty.

Walt was fascinated by the tale of the boy who wouldn't grow up. No wonder. When Walt saw Peter Pan soaring through the air, powered by optimism and pixie dust, he truly saw himself.

Canal Boats to Nowhere
and Other Attractions

Disney remodeled Fantasyland in 1983, making all the rides run at least 25 percent longer, while giving the attraction façades a major facelift. Prior to that time, Fantasyland attractions featured flat façades adorned with medieval flags, shields, and tournament tents. The tent motif complemented King Arthur's Carrousel and gave Fantasyland the look of a Renaissance fair — but the tents also gave Fantasyland an impermanent, carnival-like atmosphere.

Since the 1983 facelift, Fantasyland is no longer as Walt left it, but it is much more as Walt wanted it to be. The makeover gave Fantasyland a Bavarian village appearance (complementing the Castle's Bavarian architecture), yet each attraction has its own distinct style.

The façade of Peter Pan's Flight mingles village architecture, Old English leaded glass windows, a Gothic revival opal glass clock, and a pirate ship weathervane. The façade of Mr. Toad's Wild Ride is Toad Hall — a many-chimneyed Edwardian-era manor house. And the façade of Snow White's Scary Adventure is a dark and brooding fairytale castle. The disparate elements of Fantasyland blend to produce visual enchantment.

Snow White's Scary Adventure (originally Snow White's Adventures) is based on Walt's 1937 animated feature, *Snow White and the Seven Dwarfs*. In the original ride, Snow White was nowhere to be seen. Riders saw the Dwarfs, the wicked Queen, and assorted woodland creatures — but no Snow White. Walt's concept of the ride was that *you*, the guest, *are* Snow White. You see everything through her eyes. After guests complained of

Snow White's absence, the princess was added to the attraction.

When Fantasyland was renovated in 1983, two notable features were added to the exterior of the Snow White attraction: the wicked Queen in the window over the entrance and the brass apple near the doorway. (Touch the apple and see what happens.)

Near the end of the original ride, the Witch would hold out a poisoned apple. Unfortunately, some guests reached out and stole it as a souvenir. The 1983 redesign of the attraction fixed the problem: the apple is now an illusion projected by a parabolic mirror. Reach for the apple, and your hand passes through empty air.

Another Fantasyland mainstay is Mr. Toad's Wild Ride, derived from Disney's 1949 film *The Adventures of Ichabod and Mr. Toad*. In the film, Mr. J. Thaddeus Toad becomes obsessed with motorcars, so he foolishly trades his mansion, Toad Hall, for a car that turns out to be stolen. Mr. Toad is tried and convicted of car theft, and he is sentenced to the Tower of London. Later, with help from his friends, he wins back Toad Hall.

The impetuous Mr. Toad is Walt Disney in disguise, living out Walt's mania for vehicles. Mr. Toad's Wild Ride was originally designed by Ken Anderson and Claude Coats. When the ride was remodeled in 1983, Disney's Imagineers retained the ride's quirkiness and added to the surprises of this opening day classic. For example, instead of motoring *past* Mr. Toad's fireplace, you now smash *through* it. As the inscription over the entrance states, *Toadi Acceleratio Semper Absurda* (or, "Speeding along with Toad is always ridiculous").

(Because of its realistic illusion of being run over by a train, followed by a trip to Hell, I don't recommend this ride for little children.)

The Mad Tea Party (aka "the Teacups") is based on the Unbirthday Party scene in *Alice in Wonderland*. The ride consists of three small turntables rotating clockwise on a large turntable that rotates counter-clockwise. There are eighteen Teacups in all. The colorful lanterns and swirling colored lights are a feast for the senses at night. You'll hear the tooting, harrumphing teakettle music in your dreams.

During the first two years, there was no way to slow the spinning cups. Guests sometimes staggered off complaining of motion sickness, so a braking mechanism was added in 1957 to control the spin. The attraction was originally located north of the Carrousel, but was moved to its present location near the Matterhorn in 1983.

The Canal Boats of the World hold the record for shortest-lived attraction in Disneyland, closing after less than two months of operation. Walt's inspiration for Canal Boats of the World was Madurodam, a park in The Hague, Netherlands, featuring 1:25 scale replicas of Dutch buildings, monuments, railroads, and people.

Walt's early plans for Mickey Mouse Park called for a Canal Boats attraction called Lilliputianland. It would contain miniature cities with tiny animated human figures to create the illusion of life.

When Disneyland opened, the Canal Boats were ready — but there was nothing for Walt's guests to see but mounds of dirt and weeds. Cast members called it "Mud Banks of the World." It was literally a slow boat to nowhere. To make a bad attraction worse, mechanical problems multiplied. The outboard motors were too noisy to allow music or narration during the ride, and were prone to breaking down. Boats often had to be towed back by cast members on the shore.

After the attraction closed in September 1955, Ken Anderson led a team of Imagineers in transforming the Canal Boats ride. They created miniature scenes from Disney fairytale classics in 1:12 scale — the straw, stick, and brick houses of the Three Little Pigs, the English village of Alice, Kensington Gardens from *Peter Pan*, the dwarfs' cottage from *Snow White*, Cinderella's village and Prince Charming's castle, Toad Hall from *The Wind*

in the Willows, and Pinocchio's Tyrolean village with Geppetto's workshop.

Imagineer Harriet Burns built many of the models for Storybook Land. She made tiny thatch-roofed cottages, brick-and-stone manor houses, farmhouses, windmills, and water wheels. The houses had glass windows, and the doors had hinges and working locks.

She spent untold hours on the little church in Alice's village, creating an ornate window out of authentic stained glass, mounted with soldered lead. "I was doing all the leading," she recalled, "and working out all the window designs and color. . . . [I] cut the lead pieces, and then beveled them. I really enjoyed that. We really didn't need to do that — we could have just put celluloid behind Plexiglas. But at that time Walt loved model making, and he loved detail."

Harriet Burns had cut out all the stained glass and tiny lead pieces, and had the window assembled on a work table. Then — disaster. She recalled, "Walt came in and picked it up — and I hadn't soldered it together! It just scattered everywhere! But that is how hands-on he was. I picked it up and said, 'Oh, no problem, Walt, no problem.'" Walt's model makers learned to fasten everything down whenever the boss came by.[13]

Renamed Storybook Land Canal Boats, the renovated attraction opened June 16, 1956. New boats, named for female Disney characters like Alice, Cinderella, Daisy, Faline, and Tinkerbell, were powered by quiet electric motors. The boats began their journey by entering the gullet of Monstro the Whale from *Pinocchio*. The former mud banks were landscaped with flowers to represent Crazy Quilt Country from *Wynken, Blinken and Nod*. The new version was infinitely better than the original.

*Four of the Mousketeers — Darlene, Sharon, Lonnie & Bobby
— were present to open the Storybook Land Canal Boats.*

Walt's Imagineers made ingenious use of Disneyland's limited acreage, seamlessly interweaving the Canal Boats and Casey Jr. attractions within the same space. Though Walt's concept of miniaturized animated figures was never realized, the Canal Boats attraction contains the most intricately detailed scenery in any Disney park. It comes from the heart and soul of Walt himself.

Even so, Walt didn't expect the attraction to last. He once told Harriet Burns, "We can do this little ride, and it will be filler for the moment. Later on we can take it out and put something else there."[14] Yet the attraction continues to be popular more than sixty years later.

New for 1958: Alice and Tinkerbell

The Alice in Wonderland attraction opened June 14, 1958, nearly three years after Disneyland's opening day. This ride is not found in any other Disney park. Like the Mad Tea Party, the Alice ride is based on Disney's 1951 animated feature *Alice in Wonderland*. In its initial release, the film earned only $5.2 million on a $3 million budget. Though not a disaster, *Alice* was hardly a soaring success like *Peter Pan*. It's surprising, then, that Walt based *two* attractions on a film he considered an underperformer.

Most of the Alice ride takes place on the second floor of the east show building, directly over the Mr. Toad ride. The Alice vehicles are shaped like the film's hookah-smoking caterpillar. The original attraction relied on painted flat cutout figures, but a 1984 renovation added dimensional figures plus an "Unbirthday Party" finale at the end, extending the ride to four minutes. A 2014 upgrade added state-of-the-art animation effects, making it one of the most appealing dark rides in Fantasyland.

On August 1, 1958, Walt hosted a special event called "Disney Night at the Hollywood Bowl." He hired four-foot-ten, sixty-eight-year-old Tiny Kline to perform as Tinker Bell. Kline (original name: Helen Deutsch) was a Hungarian-born aerialist with the Ringling Bros. and Barnum & Bailey Circus. She had retired after hundreds of performances of an "iron jaw" act, "The Slide of Death."

Kline performed by biting down on a bar attached to a pulley on a zip line. She would then slide down the line as her arms and legs moved gracefully, creating the illusion of flight. In 1932, she performed this feat on a wire stretched 1,134 feet across Times Square at a height of

600 feet. When she reached the other side, she told reporters, "At last I found a safe way to cross Times Square!"

For Walt's Hollywood Bowl event, Kline wore a safety harness with her Tinker Bell costume and wings. Waving her wand, she flew over the gasping crowd, magically suspended on a wire stretched from the band shell to the back of the amphitheater. That performance persuaded Walt to add Tinker Bell's flight to the nightly fireworks show at Disneyland. But where would she fly *from*, and what would she fly *to*?

These questions were answered in 1959 with the opening of the Matterhorn. In the summer of 1961, Tinker Bell made her first flight over Disneyland. She continued performing as Tinker Bell for three years.

Every day, she took a city bus to Disneyland and gave her crowd-thrilling performance from a wire suspended between the Matterhorn and Sleeping Beauty Castle. At the Castle, cast members held up a mattress to soften her landing.

Tiny Kline was grateful to Walt for this glittering final chapter in her career. "Every night," she said, "when the searchlights come up to pick out Tinker Bell, then, up there on the mountain, I'm young again."[15] Kline continued to perform the role of Tinker Bell even after she was diagnosed with cancer in 1962. She died on July 5, 1964, at age seventy-three.[16]

Today, Disneyland uses a sophisticated aerial system that flies Tinkerbell and Dumbo around the Castle during the fireworks show. They soar up and down, back and forth, over the amazed audience.

But in 1961, it was Walt who first sent a pixie soaring over Fantasyland.

it's a small world

(Note: The official name of "it's a small world" uses all-lowercase letters. Following the style of Disney historians Jim Korkis and David Koenig, I'm using all-lowercase and quotation marks to refer to this attraction.)

Walt continually sought ways to finance new attractions. With the approach of the 1964 New York World's Fair, he committed his company to building four Fair attractions — the Magic Skyway (sponsored by Ford), Great Moments with Mr. Lincoln (the state of Illinois), The Carousel of Progress (General Electric), and "it's a small world" (Pepsi, on behalf of UNICEF). The sponsoring entities paid for the R&D and Walt later moved the attractions to Disneyland.

The most popular of these attractions was "it's a small world" — a water-based dark ride, now at the north end of Fantasyland. The ride is a full fifteen minutes long and features more than 300 Audio-Animatronic dolls in ethnic costumes, singing about global unity and peace.

Yet the attraction nearly didn't happen. Pepsi's board of directors dithered for months over the kind of attraction they wanted — and they almost waited too long.

With the Fair just eleven months away, Pepsi executives contacted Joe Fowler, who was then the general manager of Disneyland and its attractions. They asked Fowler if the Disney Company would create an attraction — *any* attraction — for Pepsi to sponsor to benefit UNICEF, the United Nations Children's Emergency Fund.

Fowler turned Pepsi down flat. Disney was already building three attractions for the Fair, he said, and there wasn't time to attempt another project of that magnitude. When the Pepsi execs told the board of directors that Disney had turned them down, one board member — actress Joan Crawford — refused to take no for an answer. A longtime friend of Walt's, she went to see him personally and asked him why his company had refused Pepsi's request.

Walt was livid. Joe Fowler hadn't even mentioned being approached by Pepsi. Walt told Crawford to go back to the board and tell them that Disney would build the attraction. Walt knew exactly what he wanted to build. For years, he had dreamed of an attraction in which children from around the world, arrayed in ethnic costumes, would sing together in peace and harmony. Now he could build it — and Pepsi would foot the bill.

He called his top artists together and told them about the attraction they were going to build for the World's Fair. The working title was "Children of the World."

It was an exciting idea, and Walt's Imagineers were eager for the challenge. Art director Mary Blair had accompanied Walt on his 1941 Latin American tour and had returned with bold new ideas about color. She devised individual color schemes for each land: multi-hued Europe, blue and green Africa, a hot-yellow Middle East, and a pink-orange Latin America.

Marc Davis designed scenery and characters. His wife, Alice Davis, created the costumes. Rolly Crump built the toys and props, while Blaine Gibson constructed the dolls. Vehicle designer Bob Gurr engineered the boats (which he later adapted for Pirates of the Caribbean).

"It's a small world" at the New York World's Fair in 1964. Over the entrance to the attraction is The Tower of the Four Winds, designed by Rolly Crump — a 120-foot-tall perpetually moving mobile. (Photo: Paul Turner)

Walt assigned his top songwriters, Robert Sherman and Richard Sherman, to write one song for the attraction to be sung as a round. This was in early 1963, soon after the October 1962 Cuban missile crisis which threatened the world with nuclear war. The Sherman Brothers wanted to write a song to underscore the World's Fair theme of "Peace Through Understanding." They dashed off a simple tune and played it for Walt. "It's just a first try," they said, "but are you looking for something like this?"

"That's perfect!" Walt said. He loved the song so much he named the attraction after it: "it's a small world."

After the Fair closed, Walt brought the attraction to Disneyland, placing it where the Fantasyland Railroad Depot had stood since 1956. The façade and show building were constructed just north of the railroad tracks. It opened on May 28, 1966.

Today, every Disney theme park has its own "it's a small world." The ride also influenced the design of such attractions as The Enchanted Tiki Room, Pirates of the Caribbean, and The Haunted Mansion.

When you visit, notice the "small world" clock. Every fifteen minutes, doors open beneath the clock face and wooden dolls of many lands emerge in a parade. The open doors display a pair of toy blocks which indicate the hour and minutes as a bell tolls.

Another notable feature is the topiary garden in the forecourt of "it's a small world." A topiary is an ornamental plant sculpture made by training live perennial plants into well-defined shapes. There are fifteen topiaries at "it's a small world" —hippos, elephants, giraffes, and more. Walt's head landscaper Bill Evans called it a "chlorophyll circus."

During a European vacation in 1958, Walt had seen magnificent examples of topiary. He teamed his top animators and landscapers to create topiaries for Disneyland. Authentic European topiaries take decades to grow. "Walt was a bit too impatient for that," Evans recalled. " 'Let's get some topiaries in the Park in a year or two,' he said. . . . The animators would do illustrations that they wanted. We blew them up to full size and then took a lot of reinforcing rods and warped it around into the shapes we needed."

Evans and his team used thuyas, cypress, junipers, and African boxwoods for their plant sculptures. "You bend them a little bit in January," he said, "and a little bit more in February and a little bit more in March until you get the bones of the plant around the basic shape."[17]

The first Disney topiaries premiered around the Park in 1963. Most were transplanted near "it's a small world" when the attraction opened. A few, such as the fanciful Dumbo topiary near the Dumbo Flying Elephants, still grow in their original locations.

Vanished Attractions and Shops of Fantasyland

Fantasyland has changed dramatically since the Park opened. The Mickey Mouse Club Theater once stood where Pinocchio's Daring Journey stands today. It showed Disney cartoons, 3D Mouseketeers movies, and in the late 1960s, *Winnie the Pooh* featurettes. It opened in August 1955, was renamed Fantasyland Theater in 1964, briefly offered a live show called "Fun With Music," and closed in 1982.

The Mickey Mouse Club Circus opened November 24, 1955, and featured cast members from the *Mickey Mouse Club* show, plus live animals and Bob-O the Disneyland Clown. Walt loved the circus as a boy. He thought his guests would love it, too (one of the few times he was mistaken). The attraction closed January 8, 1956, due to poor attendance.

Merlin's Magic Shop in Fantasyland opened July 17, 1955. Walt personally invited magicians Merv Taylor and James Hume to run the shop. A second Magic Shop opened on Main Street in 1957. (Prior to achieving show business fame, comedian Steve Martin spent three years working at both Magic Shops, starting in August 1960.) Merlin's Magic Shop closed forever on January 16, 1983, but the Main Street shop is alive and well.

The Sword in the Stone in front of the Carrousel was inside Merlin's Magic Shop during Walt's era. The gag involved having a strong man tug uselessly on the sword — then a skinny little kid would yank the sword from the stone with ease (thanks to a button behind the counter). The attraction is based on a scene from Disney's animated feature *The Sword in the Stone* (1963), based on the T. H. White novel *The Once and Future King*.

In the film, a sword appears embedded in an anvil in London, bearing an inscription: "Whoso pulleth out this sword of this stone and anvil is rightwise king born of all England." According to legend, only a person of virtue is fit to remove the sword and rule the kingdom. A twelve-year-old orphan named Arthur pulls the sword from the anvil, unwittingly fulfilling the prophecy.

The Sword in the Stone was moved from the Magic Shop to the Carrousel courtyard during the Fantasyland makeover in 1983. From time to time, the wizard Merlin conducts a ceremony, inviting volunteers to prove their strength and virtue by pulling the sword from the stone.

The Skyway to Tomorrowland began service on June 23, 1956. It was built by Von Roll, Ltd., of Berne, Switzerland. The aerial journey began at a Swiss chalet at the west end of Fantasyland and took passengers to a station in Tomorrowland (the return trip was called the Skyway to Fantasyland). The bucket-like Skyway cars were suspended from cables and ran continuously. After the Matterhorn was built, the Skyway passed through tunnels in the mountain. The Skyway closed on November 9, 1994, and the tunnels through the Matterhorn were sealed.

A tribute to the Skyway was added to the Matterhorn Bobsleds in 2015. Inside an ice tunnel, riders see a tableau of wrecked bobsleds and Skyway buckets (shredded by yeti claws), plus scattered mountaineering equipment and yeti tracks. A crate labeled "Wells Expedition" honors Disneyland's late president Frank Wells, who died in a helicopter crash in 1994. The wrecked Skyway buckets recall a vanished attraction from Walt's era.

Chicken of the Sea Pirate Ship, circa 1965. (Photo: Lee Denney)

The Chicken of the Sea Pirate Ship and Restaurant was a highly visible landmark in Fantasyland from 1955 to 1982 (it was also known as Captain Hook's Galley). The ship was constructed in 1955 in the backstage area behind the Opera House, then lifted by crane and moved to a pond at the north end of Fantasyland.

In 1982, as work began on the Fantasyland renovation (to be completed the following year), the Pirate Ship was slated to be relocated to an area near "it's a small world." Unfortunately, the vessel had not aged well, and much of the original wooden base had been replaced with heavy concrete, intended to protect the hull from rotting in the pond. When a crane attempted to lift the ship for the move, it crumbled to pieces under its own weight.

The broken concrete and shattered timbers of the late, lamented Pirate Ship were bulldozed and hauled away. The Dumbo Flying Elephants now soar over the site where the majestic Chicken of the Sea Pirate Ship once stood.

Attractions have come and gone, but the enchantment of Fantasyland endures. This was Walt's favorite land. Decades after his passing, Fantasyland is still — as Walt called it — the Happiest Kingdom of Them All.

CHAPTER NINE

Walt's Tomorrowland

"When we opened Disneyland, outer space was Buck Rogers. I did put in a trip to the moon, and I got Wernher von Braun to help me plan the thing. And since then has come Sputnik and then has come our great program in outer space. So I had to tear down my Tomorrowland that I built eleven years ago and rebuild it to keep pace."
—*Walt Disney, 1966*

On July 17, 1955, Art Linkletter hosted *Dateline: Disney* for Disneyland's opening day. Linkletter's co-hosts were actors Robert Cummings and Ronald Reagan. As Linkletter guided TV viewers to the entrance to Tomorrowland, he said, "The time is 1986. The place is a city of the future, where a trip to the Moon is an everyday thing."

Why 1986? That was the year Halley's Comet would return to our skies. (Incidentally, Main Street USA is set in 1910, the year of Halley's *previous* appearance.)

Fast forward to the Year of the Comet, 1986. Were trips to the Moon an everyday thing, as Art Linkletter told his viewers in 1955? Nope. Though astronauts first landed on the Moon in 1969, the Moon program came to an abrupt halt in 1972. There were no Moonliners taking tourists to the Moon and back.

And here's another prediction Art Linkletter missed in 1955: By 1986, his co-host, Ronald Reagan, would be in the middle of his second term as President of the United States.

Tomorrowland was always close to Walt Disney's heart. Yet it's the most frequently revised land in Disneyland — and for good reason: Events have a way of overtaking our best guesses of the future.

Aerial view of Tomorrowland in 1962, looking west. The oval at extreme left is the Flying Saucers attraction (closed in 1966). To the right of the Flying Saucers is the Rocket to the Moon attraction (note the Moonliner standing in front of the attraction). The ring to the right of the Moonliner is the Astrojets attraction. The two white show buildings, upper left, house the 20,000 Leagues Exhibit (l.) and Circarama USA (r.). In the top-center of the picture is the Matterhorn. The Submarine Voyage lagoon is in the center of the picture. Winding around through the lower right portion of the picture are the Monorail and Autopia tracks. (Photo: Orange County Archives)

For a while, Walt wondered if Tomorrowland would ever be built. By the fall of 1954, construction problems and cost overruns throughout the Park left little time or money to build Tomorrowland. Construction chief Joe Fowler advised Walt to hang an "Under Construction" sign at the Tomorrowland entrance and focus on the other three lands. Walt agreed at first, but the more he thought about it, the more he realized Disneyland would be incomplete without Tomorrowland.

In January 1955, Walt told his team that Tomorrowland *had to* open on-time. It was a daring decision. At that time, Tomorrowland was just a patch of bare ground, and opening day was just six months off. But Walt was committed to the future.

By opening day, the TWA Moonliner towered over Tomorrowland. Autopia was revved up to unleash its fumes into the air. Circarama and Space Station X-1 were ready to astonish the public. Though scaled back from Walt's original vision, Tomorrowland was open for business.

The original Tomorrowland featured many walk-through infomercials for corporate America. Thanks to Roy's fundraising efforts (and much to Walt's dismay), Tomorrowland was home to the Kaiser Aluminum Hall of Fame, the Crane Company Bathroom of Tomorrow, the Monsanto Hall of Chemistry, and the Dutch Boy Color Gallery. Three popular entertainment attractions were also sponsored by corporations: Circarama USA, hosted by American Motors, Tomorrowland Autopia, sponsored by Richfield Oil, and the TWA Rocket to the Moon.

The Tomorrowland of 1955 was hardly the fabulous world of the future Walt had envisioned — but it was a hit with the public nonetheless.

Giant Monsters and Mad Scientists

One popular Tomorrowland attraction was the 20,000 Leagues Under the Sea walk-through. It consisted of sets and models from Disney's epic movie based on the 1870 Jules Verne novel. Disney's *20,000 Leagues Under the Sea* perfectly embodied Walt's love of nostalgia along with his fascination for the future.

Filming began in the spring of 1954, mere weeks before Walt broke ground for Disneyland. The film debuted just before Christmas 1954, midway through Disneyland's construction. On December 8, 1954, the *Disneyland* TV series aired "Operation Undersea," the series' first episode from Tomorrowland. A behind-the-scenes documentary on the making of *20,000 Leagues Under the Sea,* "Operation Undersea" won an Emmy award for its intriguing exploration of the undersea world.

The retro-futurism of Jules Verne was on Walt's mind as he built Tomorrowland. This was the 1950s, the heyday of science-fiction B-movies — cheap, sensational films with mad scientists, giant monsters, and the threat of atomic radiation. Walt's *20,000 Leagues* had all of that — a mad scientist named Nemo, a monster squid, and a nineteenth-century atomic-powered submarine, the *Nautilus*. Yet the film served up all these thrill-a-minute B-picture elements with an A-movie budget ($4 million), an A-movie director (Richard Fleischer), and an A-movie cast (James Mason, Kirk Douglas, and Peter Lorre).

The night before Disneyland opened, Walt was in Tomorrowland's 20,000 Leagues Under the Sea exhibit, spray gun in hand, helping Imagineer Ken Anderson paint the backdrop behind the giant squid. It was well past midnight when Walt and Ken decided to throw in the towel and admit that the exhibit wouldn't be ready for opening day. It opened two and a half weeks later, on August 3, 1955.

The exhibit allowed guests to tour the *Nautilus* — the chart room, wheelhouse, cabins, pump room, and diving chamber. The centerpiece of the exhibit was the elegant Victorian salon with its library, pipe organ, and iris-opening viewport. Beyond the viewport was the giant squid with its waving tentacles. In the center of the exhibit were the deck and goggle-eyed superstructure of the *Nautilus*.

The 20,000 Leagues exhibit remained in Tomorrowland for eleven years, retiring in 1966. The sets were destroyed, but Captain Nemo's pipe organ was moved to the grand ballroom of The Haunted Mansion, which opened in 1969.

Autopia — The Surviving Attraction

The Tomorrowland Autopia has been one of the most consistently popular attractions in Disneyland since opening day. What child doesn't want to get behind the wheel and drive?

But, you might ask, what's *futuristic* about Autopia? We have freeways *today*.

Yet when Disneyland opened in 1955, the interstate freeway system didn't exist. President Eisenhower signed the Federal Aid Highway Act in 1956, creating the interstate system. So Autopia was a vision of the *near* future.

The Autopia vehicles were designed by automotive engineer Bob Gurr, a twenty-three-year-old genius who had just returned to California from Michigan after a brief but successful stint with Ford. Gurr was working for a book publisher, writing books on automotive design, when his friend Dave Iwerks invited him over for dinner. Dave's father was Walt's longtime friend and associate Ub Iwerks. Ub was impressed with young Bob Gurr, and told Walt about him.

Indonesian president Sukarno with Walt on the Autopia in 1956. This shows the design of first generation Autopia cars. (From Presiden Soekarno di Amerika Serikat, *published by the U.S. Information Service in Jakarta, 1956)*

Walt had his top Disneyland designer, Dick Irvine, invite Gurr to Burbank for a tour of the studio machine shop. Gurr met shop manager Roger Broggie and other

Disney craftsmen. They showed him a bare vehicle chassis with a ten-horsepower engine. Gurr measured the chassis, then went home and produced car body drawings to fit the chassis. He returned and showed his drawings to Broggie and the others.

Gurr recalled, "This old guy walks up, unshaven, funny short tie and Roy Rogers-style western belt. I thought this was the father of one of the night guards. We talked at great length about the car. When this guy walked away, everyone said, 'See ya, Walt.' I thought, 'Was that Walt Disney?'"[1]

Bob Gurr may not have known who Walt was, but Walt knew *exactly* who Bob Gurr was. In November 1954, Walt called and hired him over the phone. Three weeks later, Walt came to the machine shop, introduced himself to Gurr in person, and told the astonished young automotive designer that he was in charge of *all* vehicle design for Disneyland.

Using techniques Gurr learned at Ford, he turned his car body design into a full-size clay model. The fiberglass car body would be molded from the model. Gurr built the model in the garage of his former design instructor at Pasadena's Art Center College of Design. Students helped Gurr with the model. As a result, Gurr recalled, Autopia "was partially built with free student labor."

Once the 500-pound clay model was finished, Walt, Gurr, and Walt's brother-in-law Bill Cottrell rode to the garage in Cottrell's Cadillac. When Walt got out of the car, his jacket was covered with white lint from Cottrell's fuzzy white seat covers. Walt examined the model closely, then sat in it. He emerged from the car with wet clay and white fuzz all over his jacket. "He was a mess," Gurr recalled, "but he approved the car."

Despite pressure to get the Park's vehicles running by opening day, Bob Gurr wasn't stressed — he was fired up by the challenge. "There was so much excitement around Walt," he said. "If you're doing something out of your own enthusiasm, you don't see it as pressure."[2]

Autopia was ready for the grand opening, with twenty vehicles on the track. The cars gave Gurr and his crew fits in the early days, due to balky carburetors. He recalled, "I was constantly kick-starting the cars."[3]

Gurr learned he could take any problem directly to Walt. A few days after Disneyland opened, Walt found Gurr kneeling beside a stalled Autopia car. "What do you need?" Walt asked.

"Mechanics," Gurr replied, "and a garage for them to work in."

Within an hour, a tractor pulled a portable building into the backstage area behind Autopia. The next morning, Gurr had a team of mechanics to keep the Autopia fleet maintained.

Despite changes to the track and car body designs (including a major renovation during the "New Tomorrowland" redesign in 1998), the Autopia experience has changed little since 1955. Today, as the real world moves closer to fully autonomous self-driving cars, Autopia may become a retro-futuristic attraction — a reminder of the days when people used to drive cars instead of the other way around.

(A tip: Before getting behind the wheel of your Autopia vehicle, ask a cast member for your free Disneyland driver's license.)

The View from Space

The original TWA Moonliner was Tomorrowland's "wienie," towering over the trees, inviting Walt's guests to explore his realm of the future. Designed by John Hench in consultation with rocket scientists Werner von Braun and Willy Ley, the Moonliner stood seventy-six feet tall, just a foot shorter than Sleeping Beauty Castle. It was a one-third scale model of the kind of lunar rocket scientists envisioned in 1955 (and was less than a fifth as tall as the Saturn V rocket that launched Apollo 11 toward the Moon in 1969).

The Moonliner drew crowds to the Rocket to the Moon attraction, which opened a week late, July 22, 1955. Rocket to the Moon was a simulated lunar voyage in which audiences sat in a circular theater with a forward viewscreen above and a rear viewscreen below. Voyagers could watch the Moon approach above as Planet Earth receded below. The theater seats vibrated, deflated, and inflated to simulate acceleration and deceleration. Along the voyage, the ship passed through a deadly meteor swarm and other perils as it swung around to the far side of the Moon.

Though the effects were primitive compared with the 3D graphics and extreme flight simulator motion of Star Tours today, Rocket to the Moon — a D-ticket ride — wowed audiences in the 1950s.

Walt with Dr. Wernher von Braun in 1954. (Photo: NASA)

The sleek Moonliner replicated the spaceships shown on the "Man In Space" episode of *Disneyland*, airing March 9, 1955, four months before Disneyland opened. The episode was directed by Ward Kimball, and featured conversations with scientists Heinz Haber, Willy Ley, and Wernher von Braun.

During World War II, Dr. von Braun designed V2 rockets for Nazi Germany, though he had no sympathy for Hitler's racist views or the Nazis' goal of world conquest. Von Braun was once arrested by the Gestapo for opposing Nazi militarization of rocket technology.

Dr. von Braun became a postwar leader of the U.S. space program, serving as director of NASA's Marshall Space Flight Center. He was also the chief architect of the Apollo program's Saturn V superbooster.

In July 1954, Heinz Haber (left), Wernher von Braun (center), and science writer Willey Ley (right) discuss the "bottle suit" from Disneyland's *"Man and the Moon." (Photo: NASA)*

Both Walt and von Braun were fans of the science fiction novels of Jules Verne. Both men were futurists who wanted not merely to *predict* the future but to *make the future happen.*

"Man In Space" was followed by another Tomorrowland episode of *Disneyland*, "Man and the Moon," airing December 28, 1955 and directed by Ward Kimball. There are strong similarities between the Moon journey in that episode and the Tomorrowland attraction. "Man and the Moon" was followed two years later by "Mars and Beyond," airing December 4, 1957.

These three episodes inspired a generation of young people to become scientists, astronauts, and space engineers. President Eisenhower showed them to his staff in 1958 when he established the National Aeronautics and Space Administration (NASA). On July 20, 1969, after Apollo 11 landed on the Moon, von Braun called Kimball and said, "NASA has been following your script!"

The Moonliner was painted white with red striping while it was sponsored by Trans World Airlines. In 1962, Douglas Aircraft Company took over as sponsor and the Moonliner was repainted in Douglas blue and red. When Douglas dropped its sponsorship in 1967, the Moonliner was sent to the boneyard in the northwest corner of the Disneyland property, and the attraction was renamed Flight to the Moon. The July 20, 1969, Apollo 11 Moon landing was shown on Flight to the Moon's video screens, hosted by Mickey Mouse in an astronaut suit.

In 1975, Flight to the Moon was refurbished with new video and narration. Renamed Mission to Mars, the new attraction used a storyline similar to the lunar version, but with the mysterious red planet as its destination. Mission to Mars closed in 1992.

A replacement attraction, ExtraTERRORestrial Alien Encounter, was set to open two years later, but when Disneyland Paris racked up huge losses in its first few years, California's Disneyland had to cut costs and delay projects. In 1998, Redd Rockett's Pizza Port opened in the Rocket to the Moon building. The tailfin of the Douglas logo still defines the marquee of the building.

Visit Tomorrowland today and you'll see a gleaming white rocketship with red stripes like the old Moonliner but without the TWA logo. It's a two-thirds-size replica of Walt's original Moonliner. It was placed on an elevated launch pad next to the Pizza Port during the Tomorrowland renovation of 1998 — a tribute to the 1955 original.

Another space-themed Tomorrowland attraction was Space Station X-1. Though tame by Star Tours standards, this walk-through was a crowd-pleaser in its day. It featured realistically painted images of Earth as seen from space, painted by legendary Hollywood matte artist Peter Ellenshaw (*20,000 Leagues Under the Sea* and *Mary Poppins*). Satellite images of Earth didn't exist in 1955, so audiences flocked to see what Earth looked like from space. Claude Coats animated Ellenshaw's paintings with moving clouds, a plume of smoke from a forest fire, and twinkling city lights on Earth's night-side.

In 1958, after the launch of Sputnik, the attraction was renamed Satellite View of America. The attraction closed on February 17, 1960, and was replaced by the Art of Animation display.

A Total Immersion Experience

Another big opening-day attraction was Circarama USA, a 360-degree motion picture experience. Directed

199 · WALT'S DISNEYLAND
WALT'S DISNEYLAND · 199

by Peter Ellenshaw, the first Circarama movie, *A Tour
of the West*, took viewers on a journey from Wilshire
Boulevard and the Los Angeles freeway system (at near-
lightspeed, thanks to camera magic) to Arizona's Grand
Canyon to Utah's Monument Valley to Las Vegas, Ne-
vada, to a speedboat ride through Newport Harbor.

Ellenshaw's crew mounted an eleven-camera assem-
bly atop an American Motors Rambler, then took to the
open road in search of inspirational vistas. The greatest
challenge the crew faced was finding stretches of smooth
road (for vibration-free images) with impressive scenery

The notion of a total immersion movie experience was
conceived by Walt, who handed off the idea to his special
effects wizard, Ub Iwerks. Ub turned it into a working
technology, synchronizing the eleven 16mm cameras via
a single sprocket chain. On July 17, 1956 — one year to
the day after Circarama USA debuted in Tomorrowland
— Walt and Ub filed a patent application for the Circarama process. The patent was granted June 28, 1960.

The Circarama theater had no seating. Guests stood
through the twelve-minute presentation so that they
could turn and look in any direction. With eight-minute
intermissions between showings, there were five showings per hour. The eleven movie screens were about eight
feet high and mounted above eye-level. The theater
looked much like an American Motors dealership show-
room with five AMC cars ringing the black circular floor,
plus appliances from AMC's Kelvinator division.

Circarama USA (later called Circle-Vision 360°) was
one of the few attractions to perform flawlessly on opening day. In 1960, the original show was replaced by a new
presentation, *America the Beautiful*, followed in later

years by *American Journeys* and *Wonders of China*. The Circle-Vision 360° theater closed in 1996, and the building now houses Buzz Lightyear's Astro Blasters.

Attractions came and went: Phantom Boats (opened July 20, 1955, closed 1956), the Disneyland Viewliner (a futuristic miniature train, opened June 1957, closed September 1958), Flying Saucers (single-rider disk-shaped "bumper car" vehicles that rode a cushion of air; opened August 1961, closed August 1966), and the Skyway to Fantasyland (opened June 1956, closed November 1994).

In 1957, Skyway buckets arrive in Tomorrowland, flying over the construction site for the Viewliner station. Both the Skyway and the Viewliner are vanished attractions. (Photo: JFauset)[4]

The Art Corner opened in Tomorrowland on September 15, 1955 and closed in 1966. It sold art supplies, books on animation, and original Disney animation cels. Some cels, now worth thousands of dollars, sold for as little as 75 cents. Each bore an authenticating seal proclaiming, "This is an original hand-painted celluloid drawing actually used in a Walt Disney production." Lacking warehouse space to store artwork dating back to the 1920s, the Disney Company sold them to collectors to keep them from being destroyed.

Walt's Mountains

June 1959 heralded a major Tomorrowland expansion with the opening of the first E-ticket rides in Disneyland: the Matterhorn Bobsleds, the Submarine Voyage, and the Monorail,. Walt televised their unveiling as a second "grand opening" of Disneyland.

The Matterhorn attraction occurred to Walt in 1958. Before traveling to Switzerland with director Ken Annakin to film *Third Man on the Mountain*, Walt visited Imagineer Vic Greene. "Vic," he said, "I want you to start thinking about new attractions for Tomorrowland. Something big. We can talk when I get back."

Arriving in Switzerland, Walt and Ken journeyed by train to Zermatt, at the foot of the majestic Matterhorn. When Walt first saw the Matterhorn, he stared transfixed. Then he dashed to a souvenir shop, bought a picture postcard of the Matterhorn, and scrawled, "Vic, build this! Walt."

From Switzerland, Walt went to Germany and toured the Alweg Company factory in Cologne. Alweg designed bullet-shaped trains that ran on a single elevated rail. Walt wanted a Monorail of his own — and not just as an attraction at Disneyland. He believed that this new mode of transportation might help solve traffic problems in American cities.

After the Phantom Boats closed in 1956, Walt had a big lagoon in the middle of Tomorrowland — and no boats to float in it. The lagoon contained 2.1 million gallons of water that had to be filtered and chlorinated at great expense. Walt found his inspiration on August 3, 1958, when the world's first nuclear submarine, the USS *Nautilus*, reached the North Pole. Walt envisioned a fleet of Tomorrowland submarines.

Now he had three big ideas for Tomorrowland — the Matterhorn, the Monorail, and the Submarines. Only one thing stood in his way: his brother Roy. The Disney Company was deep in debt and Roy was determined to become debt-free. Roy nixed Walt's plans for expanding Tomorrowland, then he took off for Europe to woo foreign investors.

Once Roy was out of the country, Walt called his Imagineers together and told them he was going to build three new Tomorrowland attractions. Roy could figure out how to pay for them when he returned.

Nothing like the Matterhorn had ever been attempted before — a 1/100th scale model of the original mountain, a skeleton of steel I-beams, two intertwining tubular steel roller coaster runs, plumbing for waterfalls and splash ponds, and planters for greenery. Because of its irregular shape, the steel structure consisted of girders of varying lengths joined together at odd angles — and this was in the era before computer-aided design.

Imagineer Harriet Burns recalled Walt's confident approach to the project: "He was very confident on most matters and he would bring in experts always, but even they said sometimes it couldn't be done. And he wouldn't argue with them. . . . He just smiled. And you knew that meant he was going to do it. . . .

"The architects said it couldn't be done, the engineers said it couldn't be done. There's no way we can run two bobsled rides and a sky ride in and out, and planter pockets and waterfalls, plumbing — there's no way that can be done and make it look like the Matterhorn. Walt smiled. Then the same thing with the engineers — impossible. Architects and engineers agreed — it can't be done. He just smiled — and it was done."[5]

Perched on the border between Tomorrowland and Fantasyland, the Matterhorn opened on June 14, 1959. It defines the Disneyland skyline to this day. At 147 feet, the Matterhorn is the tallest structure in the Park (and the second tallest at the Disneyland Resort, after the 183 foot Guardians of the Galaxy — Mission: Breakout[6] attraction in Disney California Adventure). Imagineers again used forced perspective — placing trees of decreasing size at higher elevations — to create an illusion of greater height.

There is a Fantasyland track and a Tomorrowland track. Each Bobsled track has a separate queue. The Fantasyland track is slightly longer and features

204 · JIM DENNEY

sharper curves, but the ride is about the same duration on either track — two minutes and fifteen seconds.

The Matterhorn has undergone several major upgrades. I rode the Bobsleds as a boy, and I remember seeing the hollow interior of the mountain, with its exposed girders and wooden catwalks. A major renovation in 1978 heightened the realism of the ride, encasing the tracks in ice tunnels. An Audio-Animatronic abominable snowman (or yeti, nicknamed Harold by cast members) was added to howl at passengers.

A 2012 renovation gave the Bobsleds more comfortable seating, eliminating lap-sitting. The exterior of the mountain was made more realistic with the addition of millions of tiny glass beads in the painted snow, so that it sparkles in the sun like real snow. A 2015 renovation gave the attraction a scarier yeti with improved sound effects and state-of-the-art visual effects, including a frightening glimpse of the maddened yeti through a sheet of ice.

Walt's first mountain roller-coaster, the Matterhorn, inspired a second: Space Mountain. Seeing the popularity of the Bobsleds, Walt decided he needed another thrill ride at Disneyland.

In 1964, Walt approached John Hench with an idea he called Space Port. Walt had already reinvented the roller coaster once with the Matterhorn. Now he was reinventing it again. Space Port would be a roller coaster *in the dark*, with stars, space imagery, and strobing lights — a thrill ride through deep space.

John Hench assembled a team of Imagineers to brainstorm the attraction — artists Herb Ryman and Clem Hall, and industrial designer George McGinnis. They produced hundreds of drawings — and by June 1966, they began calling the attraction Space Mountain. Their concept had four separate tracks, doubling the ridership of the Matterhorn's two tracks.

When Walt died in December 1966, the company put Space Mountain on hold and turned its attention to building Walt Disney World (WDW) in Florida. When WDW opened in October 1971, the Magic Kingdom (nicknamed "Disneyland East" by some) had no thrill rides. The company briefly considered building a Matterhorn in Florida, but concluded it wouldn't fit physically or aesthetically in WDW's Fantasyland. But there was room for an attraction in Florida's Tomorrowland. The company resurrected Walt's Space Mountain idea and built it at Walt Disney World, where it opened in 1975.

The popularity of WDW's Space Mountain persuaded the company to build a second Space Mountain at Disneyland, housing the attraction in a building that is 118 feet tall by 200 feet wide. Disneyland's Space Mountain is slightly faster than the Florida version, topping out at thirty-two miles an hour versus the Florida attraction's twenty-eight miles an hour.

During the 1970s, retired astronaut Gordon Cooper worked for Walt Disney Productions as a vice president of research and development. He invited his fellow Mercury astronauts to attend the opening of Disneyland's Space Mountain on May 27, 1977. All seven Mercury astronauts were represented — Cooper, Scott Carpenter, Senator John Glenn, Alan Shepard, Wally Schirra, Deke Slayton, and the widow of Gus Grissom (he was one of three astronauts killed in a launch pad fire in 1967).

The astronauts and their families rode Space Mountain multiple times, and emerged flashing the thumbs-up sign. Gordon Cooper told *People* magazine, "Space

Mountain is about as close as you can safely get to actually being in space."[7]

The opening of Space Mountain set a three-day attendance record of 185,500 guests. Walt would have loved to see all those people enjoying his space ride. Space Mountain succeeds because Walt took roller coasters to a place they had never been before — into the darkness of deep space. It combines the screams of a roller coaster with the imagination of a dark ride.

You won't find Walt's fingerprints on Space Mountain — just the indelible imprint of his imagination.

Electric Trains and Atomic Subs

The Disneyland Monorail opened June 14, 1959 — the first daily operating single-rail train in the western hemisphere. The attraction featured two Mark I Monorail trains, one red, one blue, each consisting of three cars.

During the televised ribbon-cutting, Walt brought Vice President Richard Nixon, the Nixon family, and TV host Art Linkletter to the Monorail platform. Walt introduced Mr. Nixon to Bob Gurr, saying, "I like steam locomotives, but Bobby here likes these modern electric trains, so I let Bobby drive them."

Walt had intended to give the Nixon family a tour of the red Monorail train — but the train was not supposed to leave the station. As Bob Gurr sat down at the controls to make sure the air conditioner was on, Walt tapped him and impulsively said, "Let's go!"

Without any warning to the Nixons or the Secret Service, the doors slid shut and the train pulled out of the station. Walt had kidnapped the Vice President of the United States.

The Nixon family in the Monorail, June 14, 1959: l. to r., younger daughter Julie, Pat Nixon, older daughter Tricia, Vice President Nixon; Art Linkletter (in the driver's bubble); Walt leaning on the Monorail. (Photo: National Archives)

The Monorail made a complete circuit and was approaching the platform when the Nixon daughters, Julie and Tricia, shouted, "Let's go around again!" Walt agreed — and Bob Gurr prodded the accelerator. As the Secret Service agents ran helplessly along the platform, the Monorail took off for another circuit.

Two weeks after the Monorail opened, the Disney Company received an urgent telegram from chief engineer Guenther Wengatz of the Alweg Company. Wengatz warned of a safety flaw and urged Disney to stop construction of the track and vehicles. Gurr telegraphed a reply, inviting Wengatz to ride the Disneyland Monorail. Disney Imagineers had discovered the flaw and fixed it. The Monorail has been one of the most problem-free attractions in Disneyland history.

Here's a Monorail secret worth knowing: The nose cone at the front of the train is open to guests on a first-come, first-served basis. The view from the forward viewpanes is very different from the passing scenery viewed from the side windows. Ask a cast member at the Monorail station to reserve a place for you.

Walt's original gray submarines in 1971. (Photo: Lee Denney)

The Submarine Voyage debuted June 14, 1959. The "voyage through liquid space" attraction cost $2.5 million in 1959 dollars. The boats were built at Todd Shipyards in San Pedro at a cost of $80,000 each. The subs were originally painted gray on top with black undersides, like Navy nuclear subs. The eight Disneyland submarines were named for the first eight American nuclear subs: *Nautilus, Seawolf, Skate, Skipjack, Triton, George Washington, Patrick Henry*, and *Ethan Allen.*

Walt had wanted to place live fish in the lagoon, but the idea was unworkable. So he stocked the lagoon with live mermaids instead. In the summer of 1959, young ladies in starfish tops and neoprene tails swam alongside the subs or sunned themselves on a rock in the middle of the lagoon. Sharing the lagoon with Walt's submarines was hazardous duty, due to the suction vortex from the subs' propellers. No mermaid mishaps were ever reported. Live mermaids only appeared during four summers — 1959, 1965, 1966, and 1967.

Inside the submarine, voyagers sit on fold-down seats, looking through portholes. The boats never submerge. The "dive" is convincingly simulated by vision-obscuring bubbles. In the original version, an audio narration simulates shipboard activity as coral reefs, fish, sea turtles, and battling crabs and lobsters pass by. The captain announces a violent storm up ahead and the sub "dives" through a waterfall and into a show building underneath the Autopia tracks.

In the show building, the submarine passes a graveyard of sunken ships, mounds of sunken treasure, and several deep-sea divers. The sub retraces the journey of the *Nautilus* beneath the polar ice cap, then sinks to depths where sunlight never penetrates, a realm of luminous sea creatures and a giant squid.

Next, the submarine passes a bevy of mermaids while descending to the Lost Continent of Atlantis as volcanic eruptions shake the ocean floor. Finally, the submarine passes the sinuous body of a sea serpent. The captain orders his crew to battle stations — until a goofy-looking, cross-eyed sea serpent face appears and the voyage comes to an end.

In 1986, the gray military subs were repainted bright yellow like scientific research subs, yet the voyage itself remained unchanged. Then, in September 1998, Walt's classic Submarine Voyage closed — gone for good.

The submarine lagoon remained walled off from public view for nine years. Then, in June 2007, the attraction reopened with all-new state-of-the-art visual effects — and a new submarine scenario, based on the Disney-Pixar film *Finding Nemo*.

Walt's submarines might have ended up on the scrapheap if not for Imagineering executive Tony Baxter. Eight years old when the Park opened in 1955, Baxter was a Disneyland fan from the beginning. He started working in Disneyland while in high school, and he joined WED Enterprises (now Walt Disney Imagineering) after college. His mentor was Walt's longtime animator and attraction designer Claude Coats.

Baxter and Coats co-designed the Big Thunder Mountain Railroad in 1979. Tony Baxter also masterminded the Fantasyland redesign in 1983, Splash Mountain in 1989, and the *Finding Nemo* Submarine Voyage. Though I miss the blend of fantasy, comedy, and Cold War realism of Walt's original voyage, I credit Tony Baxter for saving Walt's submarines for future generations.

Ruins of the Future

When the Park opened in July 1955, your first glimpse of Tomorrowland was the futuristic World Clock, which told the time anywhere on Earth. The World Clock was one of two visual icons representing Tomorrowland (the Moonliner was the other).

Disneyland began a major renovation of Tomorrowland shortly before Walt died in 1966. When the updated Tomorrowland reopened in 1967, the World Clock and the Moonliner were gone. The present was swiftly overtaking the future. Tomorrowland was changing.

Monsanto House of the Future, Tomorrowland, 1958. (Photo: Linda Peach Warner Coll., Orange County Archives)

Another attraction that disappeared in 1967 was the Monsanto House of the Future. Unveiled near the entrance to Tomorrowland on June 11, 1957, the Monsanto House was an elevated family dwelling with a floor plan shaped like a plus sign (+). Made of steel, glass, fiberglass, and plastic, it was a showcase for appliances of the future.

Walt's daughter, Diane Disney Miller, recalled that her father "really was into Tomorrowland. The Monsanto House of the Future, he thought, was very interesting. He took my husband and I there and said, 'You might want to get some ideas here for a home.' . . . [But] I'd never want to live in a house like that."[8]

When the Monsanto House closed in 1967, demolition crews found that its reinforced polyester frame was impervious to wrecking balls and chainsaws. The house was even stronger than the half-inch steel bolts that anchored it to the foundation. The bolts snapped off; the house remained intact.

Demolition crews finally gave up trying to remove the foundation. The ruins of the Monsanto House foundation are still there, disguised by the current attraction, Pixie Hollow, where little guests meet Disney fairies.

Today, the entrance to Tomorrowland is marked by a small grove of orange trees. Before Walt bulldozed the Disneyland property, the entire site was shaded by hundreds of orange trees. Now one little patch of Tomorrowland has been restored to its original citrusy purpose.

All around Tomorrowland, fruits and vegetables grow in neat little gardens — but please don't pick and eat! The plants are bug-proofed by pesticides. They will later be mulched as fertilizer for Disneyland's flower beds.

The Astro Orbitor attraction guards the entrance to Tomorrowland. In various forms, the Astro Orbitor has been part of Tomorrowland since 1956, when it was called Astro Jets and was located midway between the Tomorrowland lagoon and the Rocket to the Moon. The original Astro Jets circled a white rocket with a red-checkered design. Riders move their rockets up and down as they orbit, much like the Dumbos in Fantasyland.

In 1964, United Airlines agreed to sponsor The Enchanted Tiki Room in Adventureland, but the company objected to the name of the Astro Jets in Tomorrowland, claiming it was free advertising for rival American Airlines' "Astrojet" routes. To placate United, Disney renamed the whirling attraction Tomorrowland Jets. After the first big Tomorrowland renovation, the attraction reopened in August 1967 as the Rocket Jets, which whirled around a scaled-down replica of a NASA Saturn V rocket.

During the New Tomorrowland renovation of 1998, the attraction was moved to the Tomorrowland entrance and reopened with a retro-futuristic look, modeled after the Orbitron Machines Volantes (Orbitron Flying Machines) at Disneyland Paris. The central kinetic sculpture of planets and moons was called the Observatron, and the attraction itself was called the Astro Orbitor (note the last syllable, spelled with an "o"). The color scheme was a Jules Verne-inspired bronze and red.

The 1998 renovation recast Tomorrowland as a kind of Nostalgialand. Attractions and show buildings were redecorated in a steampunk fusion of burnished bronze, red and purple accents, and neon. The slogan for the New Tomorrowland was: "The future that never was is finally here." Some Disney fans loved the New Tomorrowland. Some hated it. Many wondered, "What would Walt think?"

In 2005, the Tomorrowland "bronze age" ended, and the show buildings were painted white with blue and silver accents for Disneyland's Fiftieth Anniversary. In 2009, the Astro Orbitor was refurbished in silver and blue, with red and gold accents. Despite the cosmetic changes, it was essentially the classic Astro Jets ride of 1956, an early feature of Walt's Tomorrowland.

David Koenig of MiceChat.com observes that, in the history of the Park, Main Street has closed just two attractions, Adventureland has closed four, Fantasyland five, Frontierland six, Critter Country two, Mickey's Toontown three, and New Orleans Square none — while Tomorrowland has closed *twenty-two attractions*, two more than *all* the other lands of Disneyland combined.

The reason Tomorrowland is constantly in flux is not hard to understand. As Yoda said in *The Empire Strikes Back*, the future is "difficult to see. Always in motion is the future." In order to keep up with the ever-changing future, Disney's Imagineers have to keep reimagining and re-engineering the present reality of Tomorrowland.

Koenig offers some Tomorrowland predictions, based on conversations with "a Disneyland insider familiar with the park's current long-range plans" — plans, we should note, that are (like the future) always in motion:

After the completion of Star Wars Land in 2019, Disney California Adventure and Fantasyland are due for rehabbing (and Mr. Toad's Wild Ride may not survive the renovation). "After that," Koenig says, "Tomorrowland will finally get its rehab." This will take place, he adds, no sooner than 2024 or so.

The next big Tomorrowland renovation, Koenig speculates, could involve "demolishing the Innoventions carousel building, Autopia, and possibly the subs. Although the latter two are sentimental favorites, they cover a huge amount of acreage that could accommodate two more marketable E-ticket attractions."[9] If Koenig is right, there may soon be nothing left of Walt's Tomorrowland but the Monorail and the Matterhorn.

This would be sad — but Walt would probably understand. He might even make the same decision were he in charge today. For Walt, the future was always a moving target. The dreams and visions that Tomorrowland symbolized in 1955 have receded into the past. Disneyland must keep Tomorrowland from becoming Yesterdayland.

The Nostalgic Futurist

Walt was the greatest nostalgist who ever lived — a man who not only treasured the past, but rebuilt it better than ever. Main Street USA is a gleaming and flawless version of his boyhood hometown. Adventureland is a travelogue of his fondly remembered South American tour. Frontierland recalls the tales of Tom Sawyer and Davy Crockett — stories he treasured as a boy. Fantasyland recreates the cherished tales of childhood. Walt even resurrected Abraham Lincoln for our amazement.

Walt loved Yesterday — but he also loved Tomorrow. He was a devotee of the retro-futuristic tales of Jules Verne. And when Ray Bradbury, author of *The Martian Chronicles*, introduced himself to Walt during a chance meeting, Walt said, "Ray Bradbury! I know your books," proving he was, indeed, a science fiction fan.

As John Hench once said, "Walt had one foot in the past and one foot in the future." And Richard Sherman said, "Walt was an optimistic futurist. In 1964, my brother Robert and I wrote a song about Walt's view of the future. It's called 'There's a Great Big Beautiful Tomorrow.' When we wrote lines like 'Tomorrow's just a dream away,' we were really writing about Walt."

Tomorrowland attractions generate screams and thrills — but they also kindle a spark of imagination and hope for the future. As Walt said, "A lot of young people think the future is closed to them, that everything has been done. This is not so. There are still plenty of avenues to be explored."

Shortly before his death in December 1966, Walt told his son-in-law, Ron Miller, "If I could live for fifteen more years, I would surpass everything I've done over the past forty-five years." And I think he just might have — but we'll never know. His untimely death at age sixty-five robbed us of his dreams and goals for the future.

In 1958, Walt described his vision for humanity: "We step into the future and find fantastic atomic-powered machines working for us. The world is unified and peaceful. Outer space is the new frontier. We walk for a time among the strange mechanical wonders of tomorrow, and then blast off on a rocket to the Moon."

Well, the world is far from unified, and there are no tourist shuttles to the Moon. But perhaps if Walt hadn't run out of time — who knows? After all, he wasn't content to merely *predict* the future. He was too busy making the future *happen*.

Chapter Ten

The Soul of Walt Disney

"Disneyland will never be completed as long as there is imagination left in the world."
—*Walt Disney*

Walt was one of the most amazing people who ever lived. He had a deeper, more enduring, more positive influence on this world than most kings and presidents — and he did so entirely through the products of his imagination. He assembled teams of artists, writers, musicians, architects, Imagineers, and other specialists to turn his dreams into reality. But the dreams were born in the heart, mind, and soul of Walt himself.

We look at Disneyland today and say, "Of course it exists. How could this idea miss? It's just what the world needed — a place where parents and children can be immersed in joy and wonder, optimism and excitement, yesterday and tomorrow, history and adventure. The world was ripe for someone to invent Disneyland."

But in 1955, Disneyland was anything but a sure thing. It was one of the riskiest gambles in the history of American business. As Walt said, "Most of the people I talked to thought it would be a financial disaster — closed and forgotten within the first year."[1] Walt was willing to bet everything he had, everything he had built — his Burbank studio, his home, his personal assets, his reputation — on Disneyland. Had it failed, Walt would have gone down in history as a cartoon impresario who fell flat on his face and lost everything.

The risk paid off — not because it was a sure thing, not because Walt was lucky, but because Walt wouldn't quit. He persisted in the face of enormous obstacles and opposition.

Critics will say that a visit to Disneyland is like spending a day inside a giant cash register. Yes, admission is expensive, and so are the food and souvenirs. It costs a lot of money to build something this big, this complex, this amazing.

Sometimes the lines are long and your feet get tired. But if you have a soul, a sense of wonder, a spirit of adventure, a longing for yesterday or tomorrow, and if the child within you is still alive and well, you'll know it's worth it. You will have spent one perfect day inside the imagination of Walt Disney.

Plussing the Kingdom

Science fiction writer Ray Bradbury once asked Walt, "Why don't you run for mayor of Los Angeles?"

"Ray," Walt said, "why should I run for mayor when I'm already king?"

It's true. Walt Disney was the Benevolent Ruler and Grand Vizier of the Magic Kingdom. And all of the magic that illuminated Walt's kingdom flowed like fiery pixie dust from Walt's heart and mind and fingertips.

When *Wired* magazine asked Ray Bradbury to describe the city of the future, he said, "Disneyland. They've done everything right: It has hundreds of trees and thousands of flowers they don't need, but which they put in anyway. It has fountains and places to sit. I've visited thirty or forty times over the years, and there's very little I would change."2

Ray got it exactly right. Every city in the world should aspire to be as clean, inviting, and pleasant to linger in as Disneyland. Those who think of Disneyland as nothing more than a "theme park" have missed the point. Disneyland is the city of the future. It's a utopian vision of what every city could become with enough imagination, optimism, and hard work.

If there's a lesson we should take from Disneyland, it's this: Never settle for "good enough." Continually "plus" the experience for everyone around you.

That word "plus" is normally used as a conjunction, as in "two plus two equals four." But sometime in the 1940s, Walt began using that word as a verb. A verb is an action word, and Walt put the word "plus" into action every day of his adult life. To him, it meant never settling for "good enough." It meant always giving your guests more than they expect, more than is required. From cartoons to feature films to Disneyland, Walt always plussed everything he did — then he plussed the plus.

Disney animator David Hand recalled the epic battles between Walt and his brother Roy over the cost of plussing his animated cartoons. "Walt fought the front office," Hand said, "because they wanted him to make the cartoon for a price. I've heard him. I was with him enough to know that he practically threw Roy out of his office two or three times, because Roy wanted him to make the pictures for a price in keeping with the market returns. . . .

"Roy would come in to the production department and say, 'Walt, we can't spend so much, we're not going to be able to get the money back.' And Walt, in his sharp, peculiar way, would say . . . , 'Roy, we'll make the pictures, you get the money. Now goodbye, I'm busy.' "[3]

Walt in 1938

After Disneyland opened in 1955, Walt continued to invest time and energy in his animated and live action motion pictures. But throughout the last decade of his life, he seemed to devote most of his attention to plussing Disneyland.

Walt once said, "Disneyland will never be finished. It's something I can keep developing, keep plussing and adding to. It will be a living, breathing thing that will always keep changing. Not only can I add new things, but even the trees will keep growing. Disneyland will get more beautiful every year."

When Pat Williams and I wrote *How to Be Like Walt*, we interviewed film producer and entertainment historian Les Perkins, who related an incident from Disneyland's first year of operation. Walt wanted to hold a twice-daily Christmas parade down Main Street during December — but the accountants told him it would be a wasteful extravagance.

"Walt called accountants 'bean counters,' " Perkins said. "That year, the 'bean counters' approached Walt and said, 'Why spend money on a Christmas parade? It won't draw people to the Park. The people will already be here, so it's an expense we can do without. No one will complain if we dispense with the parade, because nobody's expecting it.'

"Walt said, 'That's just the point. We should do the parade precisely *because* no one's expecting it. Our goal at Disneyland is to give people *more* than they expect. As long as we keep surprising them, they'll keep coming back. But if they ever stop coming, it'll cost us ten times that much to get them to come back."

That's why Disneyland is always full of surprises — and that's why we keep coming back.

A Simple Caring Soul

Walt's daughter, Diane Disney Miller, described her father as a simple, caring, unpretentious soul. "Dad was very easy to read," she said. "He was always straightforward, never devious or complicated."

His tastes in food were the very soul of simplicity. Walt could not imagine a more exquisite repast than a bowl of chili with crackers and a glass of V-8 juice. He would fix the chili himself on a hot plate in his office. His recipe: one can of Denison's chili and one can of Hormel, stirred together in a saucepan. For a gourmet touch, he sometimes added frankfurters — or, as he called them, "wienies."

Walt's critics have tried to overcomplicate the man — and in the process, they have misunderstood and misportrayed him. They have looked for dark motives or bitterness or prejudice in him, and it just wasn't there. Walt Disney was exactly what he claimed to be — a farm boy from Missouri who wanted to make the world a happier place, and who cared far more about giving his audience a great show than he ever cared about money.

Yes, he was an imperfect human being — he swore, he smoked, he drank, and he was at times brusque and insensitive to the feelings of his employees. Yet when Pat Williams and I interviewed the people who knew Walt personally, not one of them ever described him as cruel or abusive. Not one. He was a tough boss with high standards, constantly in the pursuit of excellence.

Sure, he could be stingy with compliments, and quick to tell you if you fell short of his expectations. If your work pleased him, the most he'd usually say was, "That'll work." Yet *every* person we talked to spoke of him with absolute affection — and we talked to literally *hundreds* of people who knew him.

Walt was caring and compassionate toward people in need, and he genuinely loved children. In June 1955, as Disneyland's opening day drew near, a letter arrived at the Disney studio. A mother wrote Walt about her seven-year-old son who was dying of leukemia. He had faithfully watched the *Disneyland* TV show week after week, eager for progress reports on the Park. His dying wish was to ride the Disneyland Railroad — but his doctors couldn't promise he'd live to see opening day.

Moved by the letter, Walt arranged for the boy and his family to come to Disneyland without delay. A few days later, Walt was on hand as the family pulled up in their car. After greetings and introductions, Walt picked up the boy and carried him in his arms to the train station. From the platform, they watched the cranes move the railroad cars from flatbed trucks to the tracks. The cars had just arrived from the Burbank construction shop and were scheduled to be coupled to the locomotive for a test run.

Walt placed the boy in the cab of the locomotive and the train pulled out of the station for its maiden run. As the train circled the Park, Walt pointed out the attractions in the different lands. He let the boy pull the handle that blew the steam whistle.

Returning to the station, Walt told the boy's parents, "Well, we really saw the place. He liked my train." Before they parted, Walt gave the family a framed piece of original art from *Lady and the Tramp*. Then he told his staff, "Not a word of this to anyone — no publicity!" Walt's staff kept his secret. His act of compassion was not publicly revealed until after his death.[4]

Ruthie Tompson supervised scene planning at the Disney Studio and is credited with many improvements in camera technology. She worked on such films as *Pinocchio*, *Fantasia*, and *Sleeping Beauty*. She was born in 1910, and as I write these words, she is well past a hundred and still living in Maine. Pat Williams interviewed her in 2004, and she shared her story with us.

Ruthie grew up near the Disney Brothers' first animation studio in Los Angeles. As a schoolgirl, she'd stop by to watch the animators at work. Walt and Roy welcomed her visits. A few years later, Walt was at the DuBrock Riding Academy in the San Fernando Valley, learning to play polo from trainer Bud DuBrock, and he recognized eighteen-year-old Ruthie, who worked in the stable. Walt offered her a job in the studio's ink and paint department, and she found herself working on Walt's first full-length feature, *Snow White and the Seven Dwarfs* (1937).

Years later, after Disneyland was up and running, Walt learned that his old polo trainer, Bud DuBrock, had suffered a paralyzing injury and was a paraplegic. Ruthie recalled, "Walt came to me and asked, 'How's Bud doing? I'd sure like to see him again. Tell him to come to the Park as my guest.' So I told Bud that Walt was asking about him and wanted him to come to Disneyland. Bud never wanted to go. Being paralyzed, he assumed there was nothing he could do there. But I talked Bud

226 · JIM DENNEY

into taking Walt up on his offer. So Bud came and Walt rolled out the red carpet for him. He took Bud around to all the attractions, and got him front-row seats for the shows. That was Walt. He really cared about people."

Ginny Tyler was the "Disneyland Storyteller" for Disneyland Records. She began doing vocal work in radio in the 1940s, hosted a daily children's TV show in the 1950s, and became a voice-over artist for Disneyland Records in the 1960s, narrating vinyl recordings of such Disney classics as *Bambi* and *Babes in Toyland*. She hosted a syndicated repackaged version of *The Mickey Mouse Club* broadcast live from the Main Street Opera House and also performed character voices in Disney films. Ginny Tyler passed away in July 2012.

In a 2004 interview, Miss Tyler told Pat Williams about a conversation she had with Walt as they were walking through Disneyland. "I was raving away to Walt about how wonderful Disneyland was. And he said, 'And that goes for my Disneyland Storyteller, too.' What a compliment from Walt himself! I have never felt prouder in my life. I remember that moment like it was yesterday."

Walt's compassion for other people came from his religious convictions and his strong sense of morality. He rarely talked openly about religion, but in a 1949 article in *Guideposts* magazine, he wrote, "I believe firmly in the efficacy of religion, in its powerful influence on a person's whole life. It helps immeasurably to meet the storm and stress of life and keep you attuned to the Divine inspiration. Without inspiration, we would perish. All I ask of myself, 'Live a good Christian life.' "[5]

He loved his family and was faithful to his wife. Disney animator Ward Kimball once said, "One thing I'm sure about Walt — he had no extramarital affairs. He had a wife, and that was it." And historian Steven Watts, in his biography of Walt Disney, agreed: "Infidelity seems to have been an alien concept to him. In Walt's own words, he was a 'one-woman man' comfortably wrapped up with his family."[6]

Throughout this book, we've seen Walt the Nostalgist and Walt the Futurist. But equally important, he was also Walt the Moral Visionary. His films and his Park were shaped by his spiritual sensibilities and his moral vision. Film historian John G. West applauded the ethical and moral content of Walt's motion pictures:

Many of his films provided commentary (albeit subtle commentary) on the social ills pervading post-war America. They taught pressing lessons about the nature of virtue and vice in the modern world. They steadfastly — and sometimes rather eloquently — upheld the democratic ideals upon which America is premised.

Walt Disney was neither a philosopher nor a classical dramatist, but he keenly understood that good ethics are an invariable part of good drama. "Good and evil" are "the antagonists of all great drama," he once observed. They "must be believably personalized." And in the ensuing conflict, "the moral ideas common to all humanity must be upheld."

In his stories, they were.

From *The Absent-Minded Professor* to *Zorro*, Walt Disney instilled in his productions a consistent ethos with few parallels to the rest of Hollywood.[7]

Walt knew that he was morally and philosophically out of sync with the Hollywood culture. He acknowledged that the kind of movies he produced made him something of an outcast in the film community. His animated shorts and feature films won many Academy Awards, but only one of his motion pictures — *Mary Poppins* — was ever nominated for Best Picture. It won five awards out of thirteen nominations (including Best Actress for Julie Andrews), but lost Best Picture to *My Fair Lady*.

Afterwards, Walt said, "Knowing Hollywood, I never had any hope that the picture [*Mary Poppins*] would get it. As a matter of fact, Disney has never actually been part of Hollywood, you know. I think they refer to us as being in the cornfield in Burbank."[8]

The Disney Studio was not just geographically removed from Hollywood — it was lightyears from Hollywood in its moral outlook. The Studio reflected the moral vision of its founder. Both The Disney Studio and Disneyland were shaped by the soul of Walt Disney.

Walt's moral virtues also shaped his politics and his patriotism. Some critics have condemned Walt for his flag-waving patriotism and his anti-Communism — but if he were alive today, he'd point to the collapse of the Soviet Union as proof he was on the right side of history.

At the same time, Walt was amazingly tolerant of other points of view. He took a live-and-let-live approach to the beliefs and ideas of others. Disney Imagineer Herb Ryman recalled an incident that demonstrates the political tolerance of Walt Disney.

"Everyone knew that Walt was a committed anti-Communist," Ryman said. "Very patriotic and all that. So someone thought they would do damage to one of the writers on *20,000 Leagues Under the Sea* by telling Walt that the writer was a Red. They thought that Walt would fire him or investigate him or kick him off the picture. Well, Walt's answer was, 'I'm glad to know that. It's a relief that he's a Communist. I thought he was an alcoholic.'"[9]

One of the most persistent false notions about Walt Disney is the old canard about him being racist or anti-Semitic. This accusation is repeated again and again by intellectually lazy people who just can't be bothered to check the facts. One extreme example was actress Meryl Streep who, while presenting an award to Emma Thompson for her role in *Saving Mr. Banks* (about the making of Disney's *Mary Poppins*), slandered Walt for having had "racist proclivities."

Where do these lies come from? They were invented during the cartoonists' strike against the Disney Studio in 1941. The organizer of that strike was Herb Sorrell, who later organized the brutal, violent strike against Warner Brothers in 1945 (also known as "the Battle of

Hollywood"). Sorrell bragged that his organizing activities were financed by the Communist Party, and recently uncovered Soviet archives showed that he worked for the Soviet intelligence apparatus.[10]

Walt recalled a threat Sorrell once made: "[Sorrell] said he would strike . . . [and] that I couldn't stand the ridicule or the smear of a strike. I told him that it was a matter of principle with me. . . . He laughed at me and told me I was naïve and foolish. He said, 'You can't stand this strike, I will smear you, and I will make a dust bowl out of your plant.' "[11] Sorrell kept his promise. His smear is still being spread by small-minded people today.

Robert and Richard Sherman.
(Photo: Howard352 at English Wikipedia)

Pat Williams and I produced a mountain of evidence against these slanders in our 2004 book, so I won't go on at length here. Instead, I'll sum up our findings with a statement that composer Robert Sherman made to us: "Walt was sensitive to people's feelings. He hated to see people mistreated or discriminated against." Sherman added that he once overheard a discussion between Walt and one of his attorneys who made a disparaging anti-Semitic remark about the Sherman Brothers. "Walt defended us and he fired the lawyer," Sherman said. "Walt was unbelievably great to us."

Walt Disney believed in tolerance as a moral virtue — racial tolerance, religious tolerance, and political tolerance. He genuinely loved the human race, and he used his films and his Park to transmit his hope for the future to the world. This world still has a long way to go to catch up to Walt Disney's optimistic vision for humanity.

A Little of Walt's Magic

Walt's movie set decorator Emile Kuri, who also designed the decor of Club 33, the *Lilly Belle* luxury rail car, and Walt's apartment over the Fire House, recalled times he spent with Walt in the early days of Disneyland. "We used to go down to Disneyland once a week," he said. "We would sit on the porch of City Hall, which was at the entrance to Disneyland, and he would watch people coming into the park. He would say to me, 'They've been here before, look at their faces, they've been here!' "

On one of those visits to Disneyland, Walt and Emile Kuri saw two Catholic nuns enter the Park with a large group of children in tow, all orphans. Walt counted the children, then turned to Kuri and said, "Look at them all! Twenty-two of them!"

Walt leaped out of his chair on the porch and rushed over to the nuns. "Wait right here for me," he told them.

Then he ran into City Hall and returned with all the money they had paid for admission, plus fistfuls of free tickets for the attractions.

"Enjoy yourselves," Walt told the astonished nuns and children. "Have a good day here. I've made reservations for you to have lunch at the Plaza Inn, and you'll have hot dogs and hamburgers and malted milks and apple pie. You're my guests."

As Walt's amazed guests went on their way, he went back to the porch where Emile Kuri sat watching. "They shouldn't have to pay to come in here," Walt said.

On another occasion, Kuri said, Walt saw an item in the *Los Angeles Times* about a group of orphans whose bus had broken down near Fresno on the way from San Francisco to Disneyland. Walt called the studio and had one of his assistants locate the hotel where the group was staying. His message to them: When you get to Disneyland, everything is free — admission, rides, and lunch.[12]

That was Walt, through and through. He loved being able to use his Park to make a difference in the lives of others, especially children.

One day in the early 1960s, Walt was sitting in his Burbank office with story artist Bill Peet, talking about an upcoming film project. As they talked, Walt turned melancholy and he stood and walked over to the window. Looking out over the Disney Studio property, he said, "You know, Bill, I want this Disney thing to go on long after I'm gone."

"Come on, Walt," Peet said. "You'll outlive all of us."

"I'm serious, Bill. I want this thing to keep going."

By October 1966, as Walt was busy overseeing an array of major projects, it was clear to everyone that Walt's health was failing. His chronic smoker's cough was worsening. His footsteps seemed stiff and painful. Yet he continued to maintain a rigorous schedule.

Walt and Roy at a press conference with the governor of Florida, November 15, 1965. (Photo: Florida Development Commission, State Archives of Florida)

Walt was hard at work with his Imagineers, planning the "Florida project," which would later be known as Walt Disney World. He was deeply involved with the California Institute of the Arts (CalArts), a creative and performing arts university that he and his brother Roy had established with an endowment in 1961. He was producing two feature films, *Blackbeard's Ghost* (a live-action film starring Peter Ustinov, Dean Jones, and Suzanne Pleshette) and an animated feature, *The Jungle Book.*

He continued to devote much of his ebbing time and energy to new attractions. He worked closely with Imagineer Marc Davis on plans for a new Audio-Animatronic country-western music show, the Country Bear Jamboree. He often checked in with John Hench, who was developing a new Moon Buggy attraction for Tomorrowland (a bouncing ride across a simulated lunar surface; the attraction, unfortunately, was never built).

But Walt focused most of his time and attention on Pirates of the Caribbean. The Pirates ride would be the last attraction personally overseen by Walt himself, and it would open three months after his death.

October 14, 1966, was a special day at Disneyland. It was a day Walt chose to host a personal tribute to a select group of American heroes — all the living recipients of the Medal of Honor and their families. Entering Disneyland by the backstage entrance on West Street, they rode down Main Street aboard Disneyland's fleet of vehicles — the Omnibus, Horseless Carriage, Surrey, and Fire Engine. At the Main Street Opera House, Walt hosted a private performance of Great Moments with Mr. Lincoln.

Walt told his honored guests that he was personally at their service. "Around Disneyland," he said, "I'm the top kick. I run the show here. And I'm telling you that if they don't treat you right — you report it to me." Walt apologized because Tomorrowland was closed for renovation at the time: "Tomorrow is a heck of a thing to keep up with," he said. So he invited the heroes and their families to come back any time, free of charge.

That was Walt's specialty — rolling out the red carpet for his guests. Walt's highly decorated guests felt welcomed indeed. One of them, Walter D. Ehlers, a wounded World War II hero, later returned to Disneyland to work as a security officer.

According to Disney historian Dave Mason, that mid-October day in 1966 was Walt's last official visit to

Disneyland — and perhaps the last day he set foot in the Park.[13] He spent that day honoring those who had served the nation. About two weeks later, on November 2, Walt went to St. Joseph's Hospital near the Disney Studio, complaining of neck pain. When the doctors read Walt's x-rays, they found an ominous spot on his left lung.

A few days later, surgeons removed that lung. Surgery was too late to save him. He passed away on December 15, 1966.

Walt's friend, Ray Bradbury, learned of Walt's death on the TV news that morning. A short time later, his phone rang. It was movie critic Richard Schickel. By coincidence, he and Ray had planned a luncheon interview about Walt Disney.

Schickel said, "Did you hear the news about Walt?"

"Yes. This is a terrible, terrible day. I'm devastated."

"Would you like to reschedule our lunch?"

"No," Ray said. "It's all the more reason to get together. I *want* to talk about him."

Two days later, Walt's ashes were interred at Forest Lawn Memorial Park in Glendale. That day, Ray Bradbury took his four daughters to Disneyland — a trip he had promised them before Walt passed away. When he returned home that night, his wife Marguerite said, "CBS Radio called this afternoon. They wanted to interview you about Walt. I told them you took the girls to Disneyland."

Choking back tears, Ray said, "What better tribute than to celebrate his life at Disneyland?"

It's true. What greater tribute could there be?

The next time you, your family, and your friends visit Disneyland, celebrate Walt. Enjoy everything there is to see and hear and do and taste. Tip your mouse ears to

Walt's apartment over the Main Street Fire House. Thank God for Walt's life. Celebrate his good soul and his grand imagination.

And when your day at Disneyland is over, as you wave to the cast members and walk out the main gate, tired but happy, your heart bursting with memories — be sure and take a little of Walt's magic with you and share it wherever you go.

Acknowledgments

I want to thank my wife Debbie for critiquing the manuscript and helping me to "plus" it in so many ways; and thanks to my son Ryan Denney and to Karla Ortega who aided me in the research for this book.

A special word of thanks goes to Peggy Matthews Rose for pointing me to resources, improving my understanding, critiquing the manuscript, and sharing her insights and stories with me. A million thanks, Peg!

I'm also grateful to the following people, most of whom I did not contact personally, but whose books or blogs provided invaluable insights and information as I was writing this book:

Robin Allan, author, *Walt Disney and Europe*

Garry Apgar, author, *A Mickey Mouse Reader*

Jeff "Chef Mayhem" Baham of DoomBuggies.com

Michael Barrier of MichaelBarrier.com

Ray Bradbury

Randy Bright, author, *Disneyland: Inside Story*

Michael Broggie, author, *Walt Disney's Railroad Story*

Dave DeCaro of DaveLandWeb.com

Steve DeGaetano of MiceAge.com

Mark Eades, of the *Orange County Register*

Sam Gennawey, author, *The Disneyland Story*

Didier Ghez, author, the *Walt's People* book series

Kathryn Greene and Richard Greene

Jim Hill of JimHillMedia.com

J. B. Kaufman, author, *South of the Border with Disney*

David Koenig of MiceChat.com

Jim Korkis, author of the *Vault of Walt* book series

Jeff Kurtti, author, *Walt Disney's Imagineering Legends*

David Lesjak of the DIS Unplugged Podcast

Art Linkletter

Paula Sigman Lowery

Dave Mason of DisneyAvenue.com

Tom K. Morris

Robert Niles of ThemeParkInsider.com

Todd James Pierce, author, *Three Years in Wonderland*

Jason Schultz of the Disneyland Nomenclature blog

Russell Schroeder, author, *Walt Disney: His Life in Pictures*

Dave Smith, author, *The Quotable Walt Disney*

Bob Thomas, author, *Walt Disney: An American Original*

Stephen Watts, author, *The Magic Kingdom*

Werner Weiss of Yesterland.com

John G. West, author, *Walt Disney and Live Action*

Pat Williams, senior vice president, the Orlando Magic

ABOUT THE AUTHOR

Jim Denney is the author or co-writer of more than a hundred books, including *Writing in Overdrive, Muse of Fire*, and the Timebenders science-fantasy series for young readers (*Battle Before Time, Doorway to Doom, Invasion of the Time Troopers*, and *Lost in Cydonia*). He has co-written books with *Star Trek* actress Grace Lee Whitney and two Super Bowl champions, legendary quarterback Bob Griese and the late Packers "Minister of Defense" Reggie White. Jim has co-written many books with Orlando Magic co-founder and vice president Pat Williams, including *Vince Lombardi on Leadership, Leadership Excellence*, and two books on the success principles of Walt Disney, *Go for the Magic* and *How to Be Like Walt*. Jim is a member of Science Fiction and Fantasy Writers of America (SFWA).

Notes

Preface & Dedication
  [1] Jason Schultz, "On the Possibility of Knowing Disney-land's History," Disneyland Nomenclature, April 11, 2008, http://disneylandcompendium.blogspot.com/2008/04/on-possibility-of-knowing-disneylands.html.

Introduction
  [1] Jim Korkis, "Walt's Friend, Ray Bradbury," Mouse-Planet.com, June 7, 2012, https://www.mouse-planet.com/10001/Walts_Friend_Ray_Bradbury.
  [2] Ray Bradbury, "The Machine-Tooled Happyland," *Holiday* Magazine, October 1965, The Astounding World of Holiday (posted January 20, 2012), https://holidaymag.word-press.com/2012/01/20/the-machine-tooled-happyland-by-ray-bradbury-october-1965/.

1. The Walt Disney Story
  [1] Randy Bright, *Disneyland: Inside Story* (New York: Harry N. Abrams, 1987), 33.
  [2] Image licensed under the Creative Commons Attribution 2.0 Generic license.
  [3] Stephen Watts, *The Magic Kingdom: Walt Disney and the American Way of Life* (Columbia, MO: University of Missouri Press, 1997), 6.

[4] Kathryn Greene and Richard Greene, *The Man Behind the Magic: The Story of Walt Disney* (New York: Viking, 1998), 138.

[5] IMDb, "Al Michaels: Trivia," IMDb.com, http://m.imdb.com/name/nm0584279/trivia.

[6] Garry Apgar, *A Mickey Mouse Reader* (Jackson, MS: University Press of Mississippi, 2014), 38-39.

[7] Jacco van Uden, *Organisation And Complexity: Using Complexity Science to Theorise Organisational Aliveness* (Boca Raton, FL: Dissertation.com, 2004), 43.

[8] Jordan Zakarin, "Diane Disney Miller Remembers Dad: Walt's Secret Disneyland Apartment, His Passions & More," Huffington Post, February 11, 2012, http://www.huffintonpost.com/2012/02/07/walt-disneys-secret-disneyland-apartment-diane-disney-miller_n_1259421.html.

[9] Michael Broggie, *Walt Disney's Railroad Story: The Small-Scale Fascination That Led to a Full-Scale Kingdom* (Virginia Beach, VA: Donning, 2006), 20.

2. Walt's Dream Becomes Reality

[1] Russell Schroeder, *Walt Disney: His Life in Pictures* (Glendale, CA: Disney Press, 1996), 49.

[2] Michael Broggie, *Walt Disney's Railroad Story: The Small-Scale Fascination That Led to a Full-Scale Kingdom* (Virginia Beach, VA: Donning, 2006), 88.

[3] Michael Barrier, "Ward Kimball: An Interview by Michael Barrier," MichaelBarrier.com, August 2003, http://www.michaelbarrier.com/Interviews/Kimball/interview_ward_kimball.htm.

[4] Art Linkletter, 2003 telephone interview with Pat Williams.

[5] Tom Morris, *If Aristotle Ran General Motors: The New Soul of Business* (New York: Henry Holt and Co., 1997), 17.

[6] Michael Broggie, *Walt Disney's Railroad Story*, 123.

[7] Nathan Masters, "Disneyland Grew Around This 118-Year-Old Palm Tree," Gizmodo.com, April 18, 2014, http://southland.gizmodo.com/disneyland-grew-around-this-118-year-old-palm-tree-1564512062.

[8] Art Linkletter, 2003 telephone interview.

[9] Walter Wagner, *You Must Remember This* (New York: Putnam, 1975), 272.

[10] Author uncredited, "Walt's Private Apartment," JustDisney.com, http://www.justdisney.com/Features/Apartment.html.

[11] Todd James Pierce, *Three Years in Wonderland: The Disney Brothers, C. V. Wood, and the Making of the Great American Theme Park* (Jackson, MS: University Press of Mississippi, 2016), 222.

[12] Todd James Pierce, *Three Years in Wonderland*, 222-223.

[13] Randy Bright, Disneyland: Inside Story (New York: Harry N. Abrams, 1987), 107.

3. Walt's Main Street USA

[1] Jordan Zakarin, "Diane Disney Miller Remembers Dad: Walt's Secret Disneyland Apartment, His Passions & More," Huffington Post, February 11, 2012, http://www.huffintonpost.com/2012/02/07/walt-disneys-secret-disneyland-apartment-diane-disney-miller_n_1259421.html.

[2] Ibid.

[3] Tony J. Tallarico, "The Grand Opening of Disneyland," ThisDayInDisneyHistory.com, http://thisdayindisneyhistory.homestead.com/disneylandgrandopening.html.

[4] Scott Raynor, "Walt Disney World Field Guide: Main Street USA, Part I," Insightful Travel & Tours, January 15, 2015, http://www.itats.org/walt-disney-world-design-field-guide-main-street-usa/.

⁵ Dave Mason, "Where It All Began: The Little Shop on Main Street," Papel Designs, http://www.papeldesigns.com/id32.html.

⁶ Jim Korkis, "The Origin of the Disneyland Wienie," MousePlanet.com, April 6, 2016, https://www.mousplanet.com/11371/The_Origin_of_the_Disneyland_Wienie.

⁷ Image licensed under the Creative Commons Attribution-Share Alike 3.0 Unported license.

⁸ The official name of "it's a small world" uses all lowercase letters. Following the style of Disney historians Jim Korkis and David Koenig, I'm using all lowercase letters, enclosed in quotation marks, when referring to this attraction.

⁹ Margaret J. King and J. G. O'Boyle, "The Theme Park: The Art of Time and Space" in *Disneyland and Culture: Essays on the Parks and Their Influence*, Kathy Merlock Jackson and Mark I. West, editors, (Jefferson, NC: McFarland & Co., 2010), 12-13.

¹⁰ Image licensed under the Creative Commons Attribution 2.0 Generic license.

¹¹ Jim Korkis, "The History of the Partners Statue: Part Two," MousePlanet.com, November 2, 2011, https://www.mouseplanet.com/9773/The_History_of_the_Partners_Statue_Part_Two.

4. Walt's Railroad and Vehicles

¹ Michael Broggie, *Walt Disney's Railroad Story: The Small-Scale Fascination That Led to a Full-Scale Kingdom* (Virginia Beach, VA: Donning, 2006), 28.

² Image licensed under the Creative Commons Attribution 2.0 Generic license.

³ MiceChat staff, "The Unknown Engineer of the Disneyland Railroad," MiceChat.com, June 15, 2016, http://micechat.com/128561-unknown-engineer-disneyland-railroad/.

[4] Image of the Omnibus courtesy of Jonnyboyca.

5. Walt's Adventureland

[1] Wade Sampson, "Saludos Walt," MousePlanet.com, September 23, 2009, https://www.mouse-planet.com/8985/Saludos_Walt.

[2] Jim Hill, "WDI's X-Scream Makeover of WDW's Haunted Mansion: Part 1," JimHillMedia.com, October 21, 2007, http://jimhillmedia.com/editor_in_chief1/b/jim_hill/archive/2007/10/22/wdi-s-x-scream-makeover-of-wdw-s-haunted-mansion-part-1.aspx.

[3] Some thoughts I expressed in my critique of the rethemed Treehouse were sparked by a blogger identified as "Merlin Jones" (a pseudonym taken from the 1964 Disney film *The Misadventues of Merlin Jones*) who wrote a piece called "Escape to Paradise," April 9, 2006, at the ReImagineering blogsite, http://imagineerebirth.blogspot.com/ 2006/04/escape-to-paradise.html.

[4] Joseph Titizian, "Disneyland, The Classics: Walt Disney's Enchanted Tiki Room," The Walt Disney Family Museum, June 28, 2013, http://waltdisney.org/blog/disneyland-classics-walt-disneys-enchanted-tiki-room.

[5] Image licensed under the Creative Commons Attribution 2.0 Generic license.

6. Walt's Frontierland

[1] Note: The description of the *Mark Twain* riverboat ride, including the narration and dialogue, is accurate as of the publication of this book. Some aspects of the ride may change when the ride is "relaunched" in the summer of 2017.

[2] Bob Thomas, *Walt Disney: An American Original* (New York: Disney Editions, 1994), 35.

[3] Bob Thomas, *Walt Disney*, 264-265.

[4] Image licensed under the Creative Commons Attribution 2.0 Generic license.

[5] Wade Sampson, "Farewell to Tom Sawyer's Island," MousePlanet.com, May 23, 2007, https://www.mouseplanet.com/8196/Farewell_to_Tom_Sawyers_Island.

[6] Image licensed under the Creative Commons Attribution-Share Alike 3.0 Unported license.

[7] Werner Weiss, "Fort Wilderness on Tom Sawyer Island," Yesterland.com, September 25, 2015, http://www.yesterland.com/fortwilderness.html.

[8] Todd James Pierce, "DHI Mythbusters Edition — The Truth about the Petrified Tree," DisneyHistoryInstitute.com, October 14, 2014, http://www.disneyhistoryinstitute.com/2014/10/dhi-mythbusters-edition-truth-about.html.

[9] Ibid.

[10] Dave DeCaro, "Petrified Tree," DaveLandWeb.com, http://www.davelandweb.com/frontierland/petrified-tree.html.

[1] Don Peri, *Working with Walt: Interviews with Disney Artists* (Jackson, MS: University Press of Mississippi, 2008), 170.

[2] Image taken from a video licensed under the Creative Commons Attribution-Share Alike 3.0 Unported license.

[3] Image licensed under the Creative Commons Attribution 2.0 Generic license.

[4] Image licensed under the Creative Commons Attribution 2.0 Generic license.

[5] Randy Bright, *Disneyland: Inside Story* (New York: Harry N. Abrams, 1987), 196-197.

[6] Mark Eades, "Part 3: Here's How Disneyland Looked and Changed in the 1960s," *Orange County Register*, July 12, 2016 (updated July 17, 2016), http://www.ocregister.com/articles/disney-722275-new-disneyland.html.

[7] Jeff "Chef Mayhem" Baham, "Chapter Two: Rolly Crump's Odd Ideas," History of the Haunted Mansion,

DoomBuggies.com, http://www.doombuggies.com/history2.php.

8. Walt's Fantasyland

[1] Image licensed under the Creative Commons Attribution-Share Alike 3.0 Unported license.

[2] Wade Sampson, "A Walk Inside Sleeping Beauty Castle," MousePlanet.com, July 23, 2008, https://www.mouseplanet.com/8455/A_Walk_Inside_Sleeping_Beauty_Castle.

[3] Disney's *Sleeping Beauty* was approximately eight years in the making. Screenwriting for the film began in early 1951, and most of the soundtrack was recorded by mid-1953. The film was scheduled to be released around Christmas 1955, but the release was pushed back to Christmas 1957, then Christmas 1958, due to Walt's dissatisfaction with the script and his ongoing obsession with Disneyland. *Sleeping Beauty* was finally released on January 29, 1959. Just seventy-five minutes long, it had cost $6 million to make — the equivalent of a $100 million motion picture today.

[4] Leonard Maltin, "The Optimistic Futurist," video interview with Ray Bradbury, Walt Disney Treasures: *Tomorrow Land: Disney in Space and Beyond*, 2-DVD set (2004), Disk 2, transcribed by the author.

[5] Some question whether the Castle spires are clad in genuine gold. Disney historian Sam Gennawey writes in *The Disneyland Story: The Unofficial Guide to the Evolution of Walt Disney's Dream* (Birmingham AL: Keen Communications, 2014, page 80) that Imagineer Herb Ryman added a "special touch" to the Castle: "22-karat gold-leafed spires. Walt had authorized the expense while Roy was away on vacation." An official Disney Company website, MagicalKingdoms.com, states, "Sharp eyes will notice such details as . . . 22-karat gold-leafing adorning

the spires" (author uncredited, "Disneyland Resort: Sleeping Beauty Castle," MagicalKingdoms.com, http:// www.magicalkingdoms.com/dlc/parks/dl_castle.html.

For many years, tour guides on the official Disneyland guided tour, "Walk in Walt's Disneyland Footsteps," have been telling Park visitors that the Castle spires are covered in genuine gold leaf. Guides also say that Roy opposed the gilding of the spires, so Walt approved the expenditure while Roy was on a trip. The guides add that when Roy returned and discovered what Walt had done, he was furious and the two brothers didn't speak to each other for more than a month.

We also know that, in 1966, Walt approved genuine 22-karat gold leaf trim for Mary Blair's whimsical, whirling decorations for the façade of "it's a small world." This was reported by Chris Strodder in *The Disneyland Encyclopedia* (Solana Beach CA: Santa Monica Press, 2012), 225, and by Jim Fanning in *The Disney Book: A Celebration of the World of Disney* (New York: DK Books, 2015), 173. Walt also approved the gilding of the spires and roof of Cinderella's Castle in the Storybook Land Canal Boats attraction (Sam Gennawey, *The Disneyland Story*, 117).

Gold is relatively maintenance-free because it doesn't corrode, so Walt's "extravagance" was a prudent decision. As this book goes to press, the price of gold is about $1,250 an ounce, but in 1955, gold sold for about $35 an ounce. While inflation has boosted the price of most goods and commodities about 900 percent since 1955, the price of gold has increased almost 3,600 percent (for comparison, a new 1955 car cost about $2,000 and a loaf of bread sold for about 18 cents). In 1955, gold leafing was cheap, compared with today's gold prices, and was a sound investment in preventative maintenance.

[6] Wade Sampson, "A Walk Inside Sleeping Beauty Castle."

[7] Robin Allan, *Walt Disney and Europe: European Influences on the Animated Feature Films of Walt Disney* (Bloomington, IN: University of Indiana Press, 1999), 232; some dialogue paraphrased.

[8] William Berry, *Encyclopaedia Heraldica, Or Complete Dictionary of Heraldry*, Volume II (London: Sherwood, Gilbert, and Piper, 1828), DYX-DIX.

[9] John Grant, *Encyclopedia of Walt Disney's Animated Characters* (New York: Hyperion Books, 1998), 248.

[10] Jim Korkis, "Walt's Plans for Peter Pan," MousePlanet.com, September 2, 2015, https://www.mouseplanet. com/11145/Walts_Plans_for_Peter_Pan.

[11] My thanks to Peggy Matthews Rose for suggesting this insight.

[12] The Disney Institute with Theodore Kinni, *Be Our Guest: Perfecting the Art of Customer Service* (Glendale, CA: Disney Editions, 2001), 102.

[13] Sam Gennawey. "Storybook Land Canal Boats," SamLand's Disney Adventures, June 6, 2012, http:// samlanddisney.blogspot.com/2012/06/storybook-land-canal-boats.html.

[14] Ibid.

[15] Tiny Kline with Janet M. Davis, *Circus Queen & Tinker Bell: The Memoir of Tiny Kline* (Urbana, IL: University of Illinois Press, 2008), 20.

[16] Tiny Kline with Janet M. Davis, *Circus Queen & Tinker Bell*, 22.

[17] Jim Korkis, "WDW Chronicles: The History of Disney Topiary," *All Ears*, August 20, 2013, http://allears.net/ae/ issue726.htm.

9. Walt's Tomorrowland

[1] D23, "23 Moving Questions with Bob Gurr," D23.com, March 23, 2016, https://d23.com/23-moving-questions-with-bob-gurr/.

[2] Ibid.

[3] Ibid.

[4] Image licensed under the Creative Commons Attribu-tion-Share Alike 4.0 International license.

[5] Harriet Burns interview, *Walt: The Man Behind the Myth — A Portrait of a Legend from Those Who Knew Him Best* (Walt Disney Home Entertainment, 2004), transcribed by the author from DVD bonus material.

[6] Formerly known as The Twilight Zone Tower of Terror.

[7] People Staff, "Former Astronaut Gordon Cooper Helps Send Disneyland Visitors Out of This World," *People* Magazine, August 29, 1977, http://people.com/archive/former-astronaut-gordon-cooper-helps-send-disneyland-visitors-out-of-this-world-vol-8-no-9/.

[8] Jordan Zakarin, "Diane Disney Miller Remembers Dad: Walt's Secret Disneyland Apartment, His Passions & More," Huffington Post, February 11, 2012, http://www.huffingtonpost.com/2012/02/07/walt-disneys-secret-disneyland-apartment-diane-disney-miller_n_1259421.html.

[9] David Koenig, "Disneyland Rumors: Putting Off Tomorrow," MiceChat.com, March 21, 2017, http://micechat.com/155827-david-koenig-disneyland-rumors-putting-off-to-morrow/.

10. The Soul of Walt Disney

[1] Dave Smith and the Disney Book Group, *The Quota-ble Walt Disney* (New York: Disney Editions, 2001), 54.

[2] John Geirland, "Bradbury's Tomorrowland," *Wired*, October 1, 1998, https://www.wired.com/1998/10/brad-bury/.

3 Michael Barrier, "Interviews: David Hand," Michael-
Barrier.com, May 2003, http://www.michaelbar-
rier.com/Interviews/Hand/interview_david_hand.htm.

4 Bob Thomas, *The Walt Disney Biography* (London:
New English Library, 1977), 220.

5 Eric David, "The Man Behind the Mouse," *Christian-
ity Today*, November 4, 2009, http://www.christianityto-
day.com/ct/2009/novemberweb-only/fofdisney.html.

6 Steven Watts, *The Magic Kingdom: Walt Disney and
the American Way of Life* (Columbia, MO: University of
Missouri Press, 1997), 357.

7 John G. West, *Walt Disney and Live Action: The
Disney Studio's Live-Action Features of the 1950s and 60s*
(Orlando: Theme Park Press, 2016), vii.

8 Jim Korkis, *The Revised Vault of Walt: Unofficial
Disney Stories Never Told* (Orlando: Theme Park Press,
2012), 136.

9 Herb Ryman, quoted by Richard and Katherine
Green in a document called "Creative Explosion, 1933-
1946," formerly posted at Disney.go.com, now no longer
available online.

10 Peter Schweizer, *Reagan's War: The Epic Story
of His Forty-Year Struggle and Final Triumph Over
Communism* (New York: Doubleday, 2002), 6.

11 Kathy Merlock Jackson, editor, *Walt Disney:
Conversations* (Jackson, MS: University Press of
Mississippi, 2006), 37-38.

12 John G. West, *Walt Disney and Live Action*, 30-31.

13 Dave Mason, "The Story of Walt Disney's Final
Official Visit to Disneyland," DisneyAvenue.com, October
7, 2016, http://www.disneyavenue.com/2016/10/the-story-
of-walt-disneys-final.html?m=1.

Also by Jim Denney (in both paperback and ebook format):

WRITING IN OVERDRIVE
Write Faster, Write Freely, Write Brilliantly
Learn how to:
• Write so fast you'll have no time for self-doubt.
• Overcome self-defeating habits and inner resistance.
• Tap into the power of writing "in the zone."
• Eliminate writer's block. • And much MORE.

WRITE FEARLESSLY!
Conquer Fear, Eliminate Self-Doubt,
Write with Confidence
Discover solutions to the eight most common writing fears:
fear that you lack talent, fear of the blank page,
fear that you can't finish, fear of taking risks,
fear of self-revelation, fear of rejection, fear of failure,
and fear of success. Let your confidence soar!
Don't let fear hold you back — WRITE FEARLESSLY!

MUSE OF FIRE
90 Days of Inspiration for Writers
"O for a Muse of Fire!" —Shakespeare.
With more than a hundred books in print, Jim Denney has
written the ultimate book of inspiration for writers.
MUSE OF FIRE consists of ninety readings,
plus three bonus readings and an epilogue —
three solid months of writing motivation and inspiration.

Made in the USA
San Bernardino, CA
28 March 2020